Eating the Elephant

Leading the Established Church to Growth

THOM S. RAINER

&

CHUCK LAWLESS

REVISED AND UPDATED EDITION

PINNACLE PUBLISHERS

4261-40
0-8054-6140-X

Dewey Decimal Classification: 254.5
Subject Heading: CHURCH GROWTH
Library of Congress Card Catalog Number: 94-499

PRINTED IN THE UNITED STATES OF AMERICA
Second Printing

Unless otherwise noted, all Scripture quotations are from the Holy Bible, *New International Version,* copyright © 1973, 1978, 1984 International Bible Society.

Library of Congress Cataloging-in-Publication Data
Rainer, Thom S., and Chuck Lawless
    Eating the elephant : leading the established church to growth/ Thom S. Rainer and Chuck Lawless
      p. cm.
    ISBN 0-8054-6140-X
    1. Church growth.   I. Title
BV652.25.R36   1994
254.Õ.5Ñdc20

From Thom Rainer:

To
Ahkeem Abdul Morella
Your friendship is beyond description

and

Always to Nellie Jo
My wife and love
With expectation of great days in Florida

From Chuck Lawless:

To
the members of
Mt. Calvary Baptist Church, Harrison, Ohio
(my first pastorate)

and, as always

to Pam, my friend and partner

CONTENTS

PREFACE

"The king is dead! Long live the king!" For many years now pundits have been predicting the death of the mainstay of American Christianity: the established, traditional church. We understand their pessimism, at least in part. Our society has changed more rapidly in the past decade than in the entire previous century. And for many, the established church has become a relic of the past, irrelevant to the concerns of modern men and women.

But we are not among those ready to declare the church dead. Yes, some changes are urgently needed. Somehow, in some manner, church leaders must discover ways to reach a secular world while retaining the best of the traditions.

Unfortunately, many established churches have been divided and demoralized by attempts to modernize the churches toward relevancy. Is there a way to implement change without destroying the church in the process? We believe there is. In fact, we have been with pastors and other church leaders who have accomplished that very task. This book is their story. We have learned volumes from them.

Come with us on an exciting journey. We will travel to various churches across America. We will see churches that have struggled and churches that have succeeded. We will see a side of life in traditional churches rarely mentioned.

There is a fresh wind blowing in our land today. Prayer has become the most important principle of church growth. God is blessing new churches, nontraditional churches and, yes, even traditional churches. We are convinced that the revival which will come soon to America will have its base in many of the churches once declared terminally ill.

This book is a book of hope and possibility—God's possibility. We pray that it is a book of hope for you. We are not blinded to the problems and struggles in many of our churches today. But we believe that the God who created this universe is ready to re-create your church.

Joining us in the preparation of this book was Stuart Swicegood, our research assistant. Thank you, Stuart, for your diligent work and faithful service.

And God bless you, our friend. Thank you for joining us on this journey. May it be a life-changing trip for us all.

TRADITIONAL CHURCHES CAN GROW

> i am going to change my world.
> you watch.
> you'll see.
> because i have a giant of a Lord
> inside of me.
> and He and i with love
> will push through the barriers.
> i'm not afraid.
> -- Ann Kiemel[1]

The monthly business meeting should not have surprised Steve Cox. After all, he had been the pastor of First Community Church for eleven years. He knew the people well, and he loved them with a pastor's heart. Perhaps that intense love and devotion for the people had blinded him to the possibility of the events of that fateful Wednesday night.

Looking back, the forty-seven-year-old pastor recalled the beginning of the process that culminated in the heated conflict. Steve had begun reading some books on church growth. One author in particular challenged him to review the statistics of First Community Church. Much to the pastor's chagrin, he discovered that the church had grown an anemic 2 percent in his entire eleven-year tenure. Furthermore, he could find the names of only five people in the church who had been drawn to Christ from the real secular and unchurched world. Five people! Was it possible, he wondered, that First Community Church had really made little difference in the kingdom in the past decade?

That moment of church- and self-analysis led Steve to read more books, to attend conferences, and to listen to people who seemed to have a grasp on reaching people for Christ in a secular society. A whole new world opened to him.

Almost overloaded with ideas, Steve knew that he would have to design a plan to implement them. Where would he begin? Realizing that worship services were a primary point of entry for unchurched people, the excited pastor met with his part-time minister of music to discuss a new worship format. They decided to make only minor modifications in the type of music.

The pastor's announcement to the church about the change in worship went without much fanfare. The responses to the announced changes were minimal. The first Sunday of the new format was somewhat awkward but, overall, Steve was pleased. The new worship style continued without objection for three weeks. Then the criticism began.

Mr. Conner was the first to speak with Steve. "Pastor, I have two young grandchildren at First Community. I don't want them growing up without hearing the old-time hymns. This new-fangled music just doesn't mean anything to me."

"But Frank," Steve replied, "your favorite hymns were contemporary to earlier generations. We are simply trying to reach the younger adults and their families. Their music tastes are different than ours. And besides, we haven't eliminated your favorite hymns; we just have variety now."

Neither Steve nor Mr. Conner was satisfied at the conclusion of this conversation.

The next day Mrs. Simpson waited somewhat impatiently on Steve while the pastor met with a newly engaged couple. When Steve completed his counseling session, Mrs. Simpson rushed into his office and screamed, "What's the purpose of putting the words to songs in our bulletin? Are we just going to throw away the hymnals that we purchased after making such financial sacrifices?"

Once again, the pastor was dumbfounded. "But, Mildred . . . we are not doing away with the hymnals. The words in the bulletin are for people who may not be familiar with our liturgy and hymnals."

The exasperated soprano choir leader responded in a huff, "Well, I think everyone should have to use the hymnal!"

"Oh," was the only sound that Steve could muster as Mrs. Simpson stormed out.

Before the day was over, one more faithful church member came to see the pastor. Though his demeanor was calm, his concern was no less intense than that of the two previous visitors. This time the issue was the placement of the offering at the end of the worship service.

Steve attempted to explain that the response to the new registration cards was much better since the attenders had an opportunity to place them in the offering plate after the service concluded. Many people had already expressed commitments to serve and accept Christ and had written their commitments on the card instead of responding to a public invitation. However, this church member was unhappy with both the placement of the offering and the new registration cards.

Reflecting on these and a few other confrontations, Steve could now see that the outbursts of the business meeting should have been anticipated. But he really was unprepared when he stepped into the fellowship hall that Wednesday night.

The first warning sign was the size of the crowd. Business meetings were not the most popular gatherings at First Community, but this crowd was twice as large as usual. The sight of some of the faces shocked the pastor. Some thirty to forty members who had never come to church except for Sunday mornings were present. When the moderator called for new business, the riot began.

"I move that we return to the former worship format immediately!" yelled Sam King.

"Second!" some ten voices responded in unison.

The discussion time was bitter. In many respects it was a generational battle. One charter member implied that if the traditional format did not return, then the pastor should look for another church. Another member threatened to leave the church. And yet another First Community faithful stated that several families were already withholding their tithes.

The traditionalists outvoted the supporters of the new worship style by a significant margin. Steve Cox returned to his study a defeated

3

man. *Where did I go wrong?* he wondered. *How could such intense emotions be raised over this issue?* And then the frustrations of the actions hit him. *Why couldn't they be this intense and dedicated about evangelism?* Late into the night the pastor considered the possibility that it was time to move to another church.

The Issue and the Tension

The story and the characters are fictitious. The facts and the essence of the story are true. Pastor Cox's church is a composite of many churches I have consulted or visited.

The issue is that the church in America today is largely ineffective. In 1992 the average worship attendance was 107 people; over a decade later the number has hardly moved.[2] Less than one out of twenty churches grew by 10 percent or more from 1992 to the present.[3] More than one-half of senior pastors in America admit that their church has little or no impact on the community.[4]

Most pastors realize that some type of change must take place in their churches in order to reach effectively a growing unchurched population. Many pastors face two major obstacles: lack of know-how and the inability to apply known principles of change.

Generally, innovations can be implemented with relative ease in three cases: (1) a newly planted church; (2) a church that has experienced rapid growth due to relocation; or (3) a church that still has its founding pastor. Churches in these three categories account for less than 5 percent of all Christian churches in America. What do the remaining 95 percent-plus churches do? Can they be effective? Can they make a difference in their communities? Can they reach the unchurched? Can they implement change without destroying their fellowship?

Such is the tension that exists in many of the so-called traditional churches. How can the church be relevant to both the growing unchurched population and to the members for whom church relevance is grounded in old hymns and long-standing methodologies? *The good news is that the traditional church can grow.* Through my consulting and research with hundreds of such churches in America, I have discovered that many pastors are leading traditional churches to growth. I will share with you their principles and struggles. And I will share with you my own successes and failures of leading traditional churches to growth.

Eating the Elephant

Many of my faculty know that I love a good, clean joke. One of them shared with me a series of elephant jokes. One of the jokes asked the question: "How do you eat an elephant?" The answer: "One bite at a time." Later I would realize that the joke describes well the task before any leader in a traditional church. The process of leading a traditional church to growth is analogous to "eating an elephant." It is a long-term deliberate process that must be implemented "one bite at a time."

If the task before us is eating an elephant, then we must avoid two extremes. The first extreme is to ignore the task at hand. I remember when my son Sam had a monumental science project to complete. He was overwhelmed by the enormity of the task. Working together, we established a list of items to be completed and the date by which each item had to be finished. Instead of being a burden, the project became a joy because he could see his daily progress. Much to his amazement and delight, Sam finished the assignment several days before the deadline.

If we acknowledge that our churches are far from effective, the challenge to change may seem overwhelming. You are in the same situation as most pastors in America. But with God's anointing, you can lead toward change and growth one step at a time.

On the other hand, we must avoid the other extreme of eating the elephant in just a few bites. Massive and sudden change (I realize "massive" is a relative term but, for many church members, their "massive" is the pastor's "slight") can divide and demoralize a traditional church. Remember, church members who hold tenaciously to the old paradigms are not "wrong" while you are "right." They are children of God loved no less by the Father than those who prefer a different style.

Traditional Versus Nontraditional

Before we begin our journey, we must define two terms that will be used extensively in this book: *traditional* and *nontraditional*. The reader needs to understand that no qualitative value is assigned to these terms. In no way am I implying that the traditional church is a massive body of unintelligent and immovable people. Likewise, do not hear my concerns about nontraditional methodology to be an indictment against the nontraditional church.

Yet in an attempt to clarify the terms, I am utilizing this chart to provide some general guidelines.

	NONTRADITIONAL	TRADITIONAL
EVANGELISM	Emphasis on reaching the unchurched.	Visitation, primarily to Christians.
MINISTRIES & PROGRAMS	Dictated by the needs of the people in the church and community.	Designed by church or denomination with expectation that people will come.
CHURCH BUILDINGS	Increasing emphasis on church activities outside the buildings.	Most church activities and ministries take place in church building.
WORSHIP STYLE	Contemporary music; flexible order of service; variety; sensitivity to the needs of the unchurched.	Older music; fixed order of service; sensitivity to the needs of church members.
WORSHIP SERVICES	Offer several options, including days other than Sunday.	Typically one Sunday morning service; one Sunday evening service. Multiple Sunday morning services offered only because of lack of space.
DECISION MAKING	Routine and daily decisions made by staff. Major decisions brought before church under pastoral leadership.	Micromanagement through committees, boards, power cliques, organizations, and business meetings.
ROLE OF LAITY	Primarily ministry.	Both administration and ministry.
ROLE OF CLERGY	Primarily leadership and equipping.	Primarily ministry.
MINISTRY OPPORTUNITIES	Attempts to match ministry needs with spiritual giftedness of church members or attenders.	According to availabilities and openings in church programs and committees, usually for church members only.

Defining these terms is difficult because they really represent relative points on a continuum. I remember when we conducted a worship survey, some of the middle-aged adults described our worship services as "too contemporary" while some of our younger adults described the same services as "too formal."

As you examine each of these categories, you will probably conclude that your church is neither exclusively traditional nor exclusively nontraditional. You should be able to discern, however, the tendency of your church. And if your church leans toward the traditional, welcome to the crowd! Most churches in America do best fit in the traditional category. Now the challenge is to reach the most people in the most effective manner. The possibility is exciting and, in God's power, it is very possible!

Common Pitfalls

As I have gone into many traditional churches, I have seen common patterns of mistakes by pastors who attempt to lead their churches to growth. Indeed I have made many of these mistakes myself.

Lack of Communication. Pastor Cox's first problem was lack of communication. Yes, he presented the plan to the church, but the implications were not clear to the people. To use a popular phrase, the church and the pastor "were not on the same wavelength." The church must own the change before they embrace it. We will discuss this matter later.

Inadequate Response to Resistant People. People resistant to change are not necessarily bad people. They just disagree. Hearing their hurts and having a willingness to be flexible are musts for the traditional church pastor.

Too Much Too Soon. Such is the thesis of "eating the elephant." God's wisdom must be sought to discern the pace of change and leadership initiatives.

Over-dependence on Methodologies. Church growth and leadership books describe the latest cutting-edge methodologies. Stories of their successful implementation in other churches engender enthusiasm and excitement. Methodologies are often seen as an end in themselves. They must always be evaluated critically in view of the church's uniqueness and the parameters of Scripture.

Borrowing Vision. The manner in which God blesses one particular church cannot be replicated exactly in your church. Learn from these "model churches" but do not "copycat" them. God has made each church differently, and the vision for each church will be unique.

Lack of Commitment. The phrase "eating the elephant" clearly implies that leading a traditional church to growth can be a long-term process. Many pastors do not have such commitment. Some cannot wait to climb the ecclesiastical ladder to a larger church. Others are waiting for the opportunity to move into a nontraditional church or to plant a church. Still other pastors have no intention of leading their traditional churches to growth. They are satisfied with the status quo. They would rather their church remain on a plateau or decline rather than pour out their lives in Great Commission obedience.

Getting Started: A Message of Hope

You may have been in your church for fifteen years and seen little or no growth. You may have recently come to your church with high expectations, only to be disillusioned in a matter of months. Lack of vitality, petty quarrels, a steady stream of criticisms, and weak followship have made you doubt your call to the church or perhaps even to the pastoral ministry. Or you may have become too comfortable in your traditional church, realizing now that the anemic growth rate is hardly an indication that the church is making a difference in the kingdom.

But now you hear the voice of God. You are ready and excited about leading your traditional church to growth.

The good news is that your church can grow; it can make a difference. If you are committed to stay, to love your people, and to seek God's face, miracles will happen. Now, we cannot know God's timing, nor can we dictate to Him how fast the church should grow. First Community Church may not become another Saddleback, but it can be just as important in God's plan.

Many years ago, I read an interview with Billy Graham. The interviewer seemed to be curious about the evangelist's opinion of his own ministry. The question was asked if he anticipated being given great rewards in heaven for the millions of lives he had impacted through his worldwide ministry. Billy Graham said that he was not sure of the extent of his own rewards, but he was certain that others would have greater rewards than he. He said that somewhere in America today, a faithful elderly woman is on her knees praying for her little country church, her family, and her nation. Billy Graham could imagine that, for nearly eighty years, the sweet lady has been faithful to her Lord. She has prayed, read the Bible daily, and taught children in Sunday School. To the evangelist, that lady and scores like her will receive the greatest rewards in heaven. The closing words of the interview will forever be etched in my memory: "You see," said Graham, "we are not called to be successful. We are called to be faithful."

It is my prayer that this book will rekindle the fire in your heart that desires to be faithful to our Lord. If you are ready for this journey, will you join me in the following prayer?

Dear Lord, I confess that I have not always been the leader of Your church that You have called me to be. Selfish motives have sometimes surpassed my motives to be faithful to You. And sometimes fears of failure and criticism have paralyzed me. I repent of these sins.

Now I am ready, excited, and willing to lead Your church. I wait on You and Your timing. I will let You define success for me. And free me from unhealthy and ungodly comparisons and competition.

Use me Lord to lead Your church to growth. Help me to love Your children in this church unconditionally. And when difficulties or criticisms arise, remind me to keep my eyes on You.

Thank You in advance for Your victories in Your church. To God be the glory. In Jesus' name. Amen.

NOTES

1. From the book *Hi. I'm Ann!* by Ann Kiemel. © 1971. Used by permission of Baker Book House.

2. George Barna, *Today's Pastors* (Ventura, Calif.: Regal, 1993), 76. Updated with current research by The Rainer Group.

3. Ibid., 77.

4. Ibid., 87.

PART I

A VISION FOR
TRADITIONAL CHURCHES

Vision is a popular buzzword in church growth and leadership books. Indeed a church without a clear vision is one without purpose or direction. Not all churches, however, can make direct application from the writings dealing with leadership and vision. In this section we will go on a step-by-step journey tailored specifically for the discovery and implementation of a vision in the traditional church.

CHAPTER 1

IT STILL BEGINS WITH GOD

"In the beginning was the Word,
and the Word was with God,
and the Word was God."
John 1:1

The Florida panhandle coast of the Gulf of Mexico is a foretaste of heaven for me. The sugar-white sands of the beaches and the rich emerald hue of the gulf waters are unsurpassed in their beauty. The mere mention of such coastal locations as Pensacola Beach, Fort Walton Beach, Destin, Seagrove Beach, Panama City Beach and Cape San Blas sends chills of anticipation through my body.

I have the fondest memories of the summer vacations my family would take each year when I was growing up. Most of the time we would go to Panama City Beach. Sometimes, however, my parents would sense the need for variety and exposure to other locations, so we would travel in another direction. Inevitably my brother and I would endure these other trips at best, hoping that we could persuade our parents to return to the beach for the remainder of our vacation days. Nothing compared favorably to the Gulf coast for us!

Perhaps our excitement would reach its peak on the short trip from our hometown of Union Springs, Alabama, to the coast. Though we could travel the distance in three hours, the excursion seemed like days to two excited boys. After about an hour into the trip, we would see our first palm tree. The excitement would build. Another hour would pass before we took a road that appeared to a child as a narrow path in a dense forest of pine trees. On each side of the road, the trees would obstruct our view except for that which was directly in front of us.

13

Finally we would see a road sign that encouraged us that the beaches were ten miles ahead. We would strain to see any sign of their white beauty. But even when we were less than a mile away, our view would be obstructed by buildings and coastal motels. Not until we were almost directly upon the beach could we see the sand and waves. Our destination was complete!

Discovering God's vision for your traditional church can be like traveling a road strewn with obstacles. Just when we think we might see the right direction or the right ministry for the church, our vision-view is obstructed by another barrier or obstacle. We relate well to the Israelites who wandered forty years in a wilderness before entering the promised land.

In this chapter we will take our first step of the journey in discovering God's vision for the traditional church. This initial step will be the most important and, perhaps, the most difficult. This leg of the journey addresses your relationship to your church, to other people, and, most importantly, to God.

On my shelves are rows of church growth and leadership books. I have attended dozens of church growth conferences. In some cases one could get the impression from these resources that the secret to growing a church is a proper mixture and order of methodologies and programs. References to God and His sovereignty are infrequent and, in a few cases, absent.

None of these church growth leaders deliberately overlooks the importance of prayer and submission to our Lord. But methodologies are perhaps overemphasized. As we begin our excursion toward discovering the vision for our churches, we must remember that it is God's vision and not our own. And like my brother and me, who had too many obstacles to see the beach, our view of God's vision also will be obstructed at times. In the traditional church, some factors will contribute to our discovering God's plan, while others will hinder the process. Understanding these pathways and obstacles is a good place to begin.

Vision Pathways/ Vision Obstacles

Can you imagine a business that opens its doors each day uncertain of its product or service? "Will we sell televisions today or will we

14

cook hamburgers?" a confused manager might ask. Is such a scenario realistic? Of course not! Businesses understand their product, how that product is made, and to whom the product will be sold.

Yet it is amazing that the most important organization (and organism) on earth, the church, is often the most confused about its purpose and particular vision for carrying out that purpose. Perhaps some church members could express that the church is in the "business" of evangelism, worship, ministry, and discipleship.[1] But very few members, including church staff, could articulate how these purposes will be specifically accomplished by the church in its local context. It is the discovery of this "how" that establishes the vision for your church.

Moses knew his purpose in the leadership of the people of Israel. He would lead them out of Egypt through the Sinai Peninsula to the promised land. But it took God's presence in a cloud and a pillar of fire for Moses to understand the specific path that Israel would take. In a traditional church, the specifics of God's vision can be discovered. In fact, in your church today are some resources that can be among your chief allies in the discovery process. These allies are called "vision pathways."

Vision Pathways

In our vacations to the beach, my brother and I were often frustrated by the obstacles that blocked our view of the beach. But had it not been for well-built roads and a dependable automobile, the sight of the beaches would have never come to fruition. In your church today are some pathways without which the vision may never be realized.

Stability. Most traditional churches have at least a core group of people who can be depended on in good times and bad. They are not fair-weather Christians ready to leave at the first sign of difficulty. In many towns and cities, it is not unusual to have one or two churches that are the centers of excitement or newness. Other churches in town lose members to these churches as "sheep-shuffling" takes place. Since most all churches have life cycles which involve growth and decline, today's new and exciting church may be tomorrow's slower-growth traditional church. It is that tenacious core group that provides the

15

traditional church a sense of stability and through which the vision can continue or be revitalized.

Koinonia. Just a few weeks before I began writing this book, a twenty-year-old church member was killed in an automobile accident. She had grown up in our church and had been active in our youth ministry. Her parents were also longtime Sunday School teachers.

When I arrived at their home, countless church members had already arrived. Some were bringing food for meals. One was on the telephone, carrying out the family's requests for arrangements. Several were greeting people as they arrived. Perhaps the most touching sight was taking place outside. Bob Finley, the most beloved high school football coach in our state and a member of our church, was mowing the lawn and doing other yardwork. He could not express his grief and sympathy in words, so he did what he does best: being a Christlike servant for others.

Such a bond between Christians is called *koinonia* in the New Testament. We usually translate the word as "fellowship," although the full depth of the meaning means much more. The word implies a deep level of commitment of Christians one to another. The commitment not only has depth, but longevity as well. Many traditional churches are beautiful examples of New Testament *koinonia*. If a vision is to be really caught and taught in a local church, it must happen among Christians who are not only committed to their Lord, but to their brothers and sisters in Christ as well.

Love of Church. Another requisite pathway for a vision to become a reality in a church is for the people to love their church. How far should that love go? When Paul wrote to the church at Colossae, he rejoiced that his love for the people resulted in suffering (Col. 1:24), servanthood (v. 25), and struggles (2:1). He had no shallow affection for Christ's church. Indeed he was willing to pour out his life for the sake of the church (2 Tim. 4:6).

In a traditional church it is not unusual to see a dedicated group of people whose love for the church is a testimony to others. A vision will never take hold in a church where love does not abound. Indeed one of the keys to communicating God's vision for a church is to help the people understand that they can demonstrate true love by carrying out the vision.

16

Hard Workers. On a given day at many traditional churches you will see lay Christians almost live at the church, working on the physical facilities, decorating, checking on our financial situation, taking sermon tapes to homebound members, and being available for other requests. They not only love their church; they demonstrate that love in action.

Carrying out a church's vision is hard work. It requires a group of people who will give sacrificially of their labor, time, prayers, and money. I recently studied about fifty churches whose age and demographic potential were similar. As best as I could, I divided the churches into two categories: traditional and nontraditional. Contrary to my expectations, the traditional churches exceeded the nontraditional churches in baptismal ratio (baptisms per resident members) and per capita giving. Such a study, even if it included much more data, cannot be conclusive about church commitment and the sacrificial attitude of the members. It can, however, point to a potential pathway for the vision to become a reality in the traditional church.

Tradition Bearers. Tradition is the handing down or continuing of beliefs, customs, and practices. Tradition is not a qualitative term. It can be good, bad, or neutral. A family whose children carry on the tradition of bank robbery are obviously handing down immoral values. On the other hand, for a family who has been practicing benevolent acts in a community for generations, the traditions are healthy and good.

Tradition bearers in a church can be positive factors for carrying forth the vision. When our church sensed God leading us to establish a new church, we turned to one of the oldest members for encouragement. Helen Bell stood before the church and told the people that Green Valley Baptist Church had been started some thirty years earlier by Philadelphia Baptist Church. She then admonished us with the reminder that we were founded as a daughter church that we too might give birth to other churches. A valued tradition became the foundation for the future vision.

Prayer Warriors. Although I cannot explain this phenomenon, it is a truism with few exceptions. Traditional churches seem to be blessed with one or more prayer warriors. When I speak of prayer warriors, I am not speaking of people who are simply faithful in their prayer lives.

I refer to people whose days are consumed with prayer, for whom prayer is the very essence of their being, for whom prayer is a passion. And if the vision for a traditional church begins with God, then the first step is bathing the vision in constant, fervent prayer.

I think of the prayer warriors I have known and loved: Lillian Anderson, Azalea Baptist Church in St. Petersburg, Florida; Ruth Emfinger in First Baptist Church of Union Springs, Alabama; and Aulene Maxwell in Birmingham, Alabama. These ladies follow in the footsteps of such prayer warriors as John "Praying" Hyde and Andrew Murray. When God places in your church a person of prayer, He is opening the door for vision discovery and vision implementation. Prayer warriors should be among the first people to be included in the process.

Vision Obstacles

While the traditional church has several wonderful resources which are invaluable in the process of vision discovery and implementation, certain vision obstacles are common as well. In part 3 of this book, we will look in detail at four major obstacles for traditional churches and possible solutions. For now, we will briefly examine some of the obstacles which obstruct the view of the vision.

Koinonitis. C. Peter Wagner coined the word *koinonitis* to describe a sick fellowship group.[2] The group no longer has an outward focus. Its primary concern is the preservation of the existing group. Outsiders are not welcome.

A problem with groups suffering from *koinonitis* is that they often do not realize that they are unfriendly to outsiders. My wife Jo once visited a church where she heard about a "super-friendly" Sunday School class. Out of curiosity, she decided to arrive on time and sit on the front row of the rather large class. At exactly the time class was to begin, Jo was the only one present! Over the next thirty minutes, thirty-five people, including the teacher, walked into the class, but no one spoke to my wife or acknowledged her presence. Friendly class? In the eyes of the class members, they were friendly. The problem is that they restricted their friendliness to those within their group. *Koinonitis* can infect any group, and the disease ultimately affects the entire church.

18

Resistance to Change. The very nature of a vision is that it leads a church to a point beyond the status quo. Such a process always engenders change. Resistance to change is common to churches that have been in a familiar and comfortable pattern. We will address this issue more thoroughly in chapter 10.

Power Groups. The very factor that engenders stability in a traditional church can also cause niches of power to develop. A particular family may have a long history in the church and perceive that they must make all the decisions for "their" church. Or a group such as a deacon body or finance committee may have stability to the point that no fresh ideas by newer people have been introduced to the group.

In such situations it is not unusual for the power groups to protect their authority. They usually mean well, but they have difficulty believing that a newer person could know the church and love the church as much as they do. Their authority, therefore, is perceived to be the best for the church.

Uncertain Focus and Direction. The story takes place in an unknown island country at the beginning of this century. An American who happened to dock his boat on the island discovered a peculiar farming practice of the native islanders. The farmers plowed their fields with a mule-driven plow in an unusual pattern. Instead of straight lines, the mules were forced to drag the plow in an awkward and difficult zig-zag pattern. Upon closer inspection, the American discovered that large rocks were placed in the field which caused the farmer to move around the obstacles. Each year the farmers would place the rocks in the field and then proceed with their planning.

The American questioned the well-meaning farmers who could only answer with the infamous statement: "We've always done it that way." The curious American was able to find some hieroglyphic writings which had not been uncovered for a century. The native islanders were stunned when the symbols explained the origin of the strange farming practice.

It seems that when the first few families arrived on the island, a small animal lived underneath the most fertile fields. When his homestead was disturbed, the animal responded angrily by destroying the newly plowed field. The first farmers soon discovered that a stone temporarily placed over the entrance to the underground dwelling kept the cantankerous animal from being bothered by the above-ground activity. As soon as the ground was plowed around the stones, the rocks were removed from the fields.

For a century this practice had continued. But the oldest islander recalled that the animal had not been seen for sixty years! The practice of setting and removing the stones had continued simply because "that's the way we have always done it."

For many traditional churches, programs, methodologies, schedules, and organizations exist because "that's the way we have always done it." God's vision is not seen clearly because new wine cannot be poured into old wineskins.

Majoring on Minors. When a traditional church loses its direction and focus, relatively insignificant items grow in importance to the detriment of the real important needs. Budgets and bills become more important than souls and eternity. The order of worship becomes more important than the hours of prayer. And constitutions and by-laws provide more leadership than the Holy Spirit.

Institutional Survival. When the church is more concerned about the survival of the institution than its purpose and mission, an inward focus develops. Decisions may be made on the basis of financial feasibility rather than God's direction. While good stewardship should certainly guide the decision-making process, the key question is: What would God have us to do?

The Struggling Pastor

Thousands of pastors and other church leaders are in traditional churches of all sizes in many locations. Most of them desire growth and a renewed vision for the church. And yet hardly a day goes by that I do not talk to a pastor who is struggling, but desiring to see his ministry make a difference for the kingdom.

The median age of pastors in America is forty-four.[3] Only 6 percent of all pastors are sixty-five or older.[4] Retirement by the age of sixty-five "is not an admission of defeat but a welcome respite from the pressures of full-time pastoral duty."[5] And in 70 percent of the churches in America, the pastor is the only full-time staff person.[6] In this environment he is often expected to be omnipotent, omnipresent, and omniscient.

It is little wonder that many pastors have such little emotional reserves to lead a church in the discovery and implementation of its vision. Barna says it well: "Ministry is tough work, and thousands of pastors bear the scars to prove it. Although many lay leaders idealize the work of the clergy, the harsh reality is that despite the best efforts of these learned individuals and regardless of the high and holy nature of the calling, pastoring a church is more burdensome than most people realize."[7]

If you are a pastor or church leader who understands well the reality of the previous sentence, you may have serious doubts about your ability to lead a church toward a new vision. You may agree with some of the pundits who have declared the demise of the effective traditional church.

I am not, however, ready to write the obituary of 90 percent of the churches in America. Certainly some changes must take place for more of these churches to be effective, but determining the extent and pace of these changes requires wisdom from God. For most pastors, the process will be painfully slow, "one bite at a time." And the first "bite," the first step, will be directed to the pastor. If you are really ready to discover and implement God's vision in your church, it begins with you, the pastor. Or better stated, it begins with God as He works in you and through your ministry.

If you are indeed willing to take the first step, I invite you to read the next ten questions. The questions are hard-hitting but necessary. Leading a traditional church to growth is a laborious task, but the rewards can be many. The relationship between the pastor and God is a critical first step in a long-term process.

Ten Tough Questions

The vision begins with God, but God works through His leaders. Is anything interfering in your relationship with God? Perhaps in a quiet place, you can answer these questions honestly in the presence of your Lord.

21

1. How Is Your Prayer Life?

Aulene Maxwell, the earlier-mentioned prayer warrior, caught me off guard with her declaration to me: "Pastor, God has great plans for you, but nothing will happen unless you pray." Now, I know Aulene well enough not to be offended by her blunt comments. And she was right! My time in prayer had dwindled considerably. It just seemed as if I had too many "important" things to do.

Pastors, church leaders, let us get painfully honest with each other and with God. Most of us have so many demands on our lives that prayer takes a back seat to everything else. Recent studies have shown that the average American pastor spends from fifteen to twenty-two minutes daily in prayer. And one of four pastors spends less than ten minutes daily in prayer.

If you expected to purchase this book to find some magical formula to lead a traditional church to growth, you are in for a disappointment. The methodologies described in the following pages are slow and laborious. But even before the methodologies are initiated, everything you do and say must begin with God.

In this first chapter, we begin describing the process by which you can lead your traditional church to discover God's *plan* for fellowship. The key is that it is God's plan and not your own. *Expect* failure if you are not a person of prayer. How can we hear God's voice if we are not listening? A study of churches that were previously plateaued or declining but now experiencing growth revealed a fascinating statistic. The report concluded that "71 percent of [these] churches reported an increased emphasis on prayer over the past several years as compared to only 40 percent of churches which continue on the plateau."[8]

A small group of believers in the first Christian church "joined together constantly in prayers" (Acts 1:14). The prayers of the early church unleashed the power of God to add thousands to the church. It happened then. It is happening today in some traditional churches once thought to be at death's door. It can happen in your church if your people are praying, but do not expect others to have a priority of prayer unless you are first sold out. How is your prayer life?

2. Whom Did You Tell about Jesus Today?

Michael actually made the appointment to see me. I wish I could say the initiative was mine, but it was not. For almost two hours he told me about his childhood in a large midwestern city. His parents never attended church, nor did they try to influence their children in any religious direction. By his own admission, Michael was a "searching agnostic."

He came to our church as a result of his marriage. Michael met Linda, one of our church members, and eventually married her. They made the decision to move to her hometown. After they had their first child, Michael began to think seriously about the faith that was missing in his life. He desired a different life for his daughter. So he came to talk to me. Michael had so many honest but tough questions, and he encouraged me to tell him about Jesus and the way of salvation.

I have heard it said often that the laity in our church must do the witnessing since they are the ones who have regular contact with non-Christians. Such a statement is true, but I am afraid that many vocational ministers use that truth as a convenient excuse not to witness. The reality is that we may have more opportunities because of our position. Regardless, God will honor our prayers if we ask Him for witnessing opportunities.

You are probably sincere in your desire to see God's vision for your church. Vision is an outward focus of God's possibilities. Can we really expect Him to show us that vision unless we are outwardly focused ourselves? Whom did you tell about Jesus today?

3. How Is Your Family Life?

A wise pastor offered me one bit of advice when I shared with him that God had called me to be a pastor. "Do not neglect your family," he said. "You will live to regret it." I conveniently forgot his words of wisdom when I accepted the call to pastor my first church.

Perhaps I rationalized my absence from my family. I was a full-time student at seminary; I worked thirty hours a week at a bank; and I was the pastor of a small church. After one particularly exhausting day, I entered our small apartment. The time was 10:00 P.M. The first words I heard upon walking in the door came from my five-year-old son:

"Daddy, Daddy, come here!" My temper began to rise as I grumbled that my son should be in bed and asleep.

Instead of waiting for Sam to speak, I began to yell at my son: "Sam, what are you doing awake? Don't you know it's past your bedtime?" For the longest few seconds, silence engulfed the room. Enough light came through the partially opened door for me to see the tears streaming down Sam's face. Finally he whispered, "I'm sorry Daddy. I just haven't seen you in so long. I decided to stay awake until you got home so that I could hug you and tell you that I love you."

If the Lord Jesus Christ had spoken those words, I would not have been more convicted. I asked my little fellow for forgiveness. His words? "Sure, Daddy, I forgive you. And Jesus does, too." With his little arm around my shoulder, I dropped to my knees, asked the Lord for forgiveness, and dedicated my life anew to my family.

My family life has not been perfect since that moment in 1985, but the commitment is still genuine today. Do you remember Paul's word to a young pastor named Timothy? "If anyone does not know how to manage his own family, how can he take care of God's church?" (1 Tim. 3:5). Wow! Those words are powerful! God will reveal His vision for your traditional church after you have your family priorities in order. How is your family life?

4. Do You Need to Reconcile with Someone?

Imagine that you are praying to God to reveal His vision for your church. You are burdened to discover how your traditional church can make a difference for the kingdom. In the midst of your request, you hear the voice of God say "No, way!" You would be shocked to say the least.

Though such a scenario may not be completely accurate, the theological truth is on target. Jesus said, "Therefore, if you are offering your gift at the altar and there remember that your brother has something against you, leave your gift there in front of the altar. First go and be reconciled to your brother; then come and offer your gift" (Matt. 5:23-24). At another point Jesus said, "But if you do not forgive men their sins, your Father will not forgive your sins" (6:15).

Jesus obviously placed a high value on the relationships between Christians. In fact, God refuses to accept our worship and service until we are in right relationship with others. Perhaps the reason we sense that our churches are stagnant is that we have a broken relationship that needs healing. Do you need to reconcile with someone?

5. Are You Handling Your Finances Biblically?

If you have read a book by such Christian financial authorities as Larry Burkett or Ron Blue, you already know that money is a dominating topic in the Bible. On the one hand, Paul admonishes churches to make certain that their ministers are compensated adequately (1 Tim. 3:17-18). On the other hand, Jesus warns all Christians that a preoccupation with the material world precludes our having a focus on the important matters of God (cf. Matt. 6:19-21).

Too many ministers are poorly compensated. If you are a layperson reading this book, I encourage you to talk frankly with your pastor or other staff persons. Ask them to be honest with you about their financial needs. If they express a need, go to those authorities in your church who could do something about the compensation level. A pastor or other staff member cannot be a visionary leader if his or her emotional reserves are consumed with worry over paying bills.

How well my wife and I know such a scenario. Many years ago, we unwisely incurred some seminary-education debt that was straining our budget. Even without the debt, my compensation as church pastor barely met the monthly bills of my family of five. I finally accepted the call to another church and, I must confess, the financial needs played a major role in our decision.

I learned two important lessons from this difficult time. First, incurring debt can be poor stewardship. While the Bible does not specifically prohibit incurring debt, it provides several warnings against it. My wife and I made a commitment to get out of debt, a process that took four years and many prayers. Second, I learned that pride kept me from asking for help. After I accepted the call to the new church, one person in the church I was leaving came to see me. She suspected that my leaving had some financial implications. I hesitatingly confirmed it. "If you only had shared your needs with us, Thom," she said, "we would have helped."

Sometimes, however, it is not the level of compensation that is the problem. Rather it is our handling of the money. Is your lifestyle one that honors Christ? Could you make some adjustments to downscale your lifestyle? Do you give abundantly and cheerfully, well beyond the tithe? Do you have a budget so that you can manage your money well? Do you incur as little debt as possible? Are you handling your finances biblically?

6. Are You Committed to Stay?

Any role of leadership should be viewed with a long-term outlook. "Quick-fix" solutions usually do more harm than good. Long-term commitments are desperately needed in traditional churches. But the average tenure of pastors has declined from seven years to four years in the past twenty years.[9] Among some denomination's pastors, the average tenure is even shorter.

While pastors are leaving churches at a more rapid pace than ever, numerous studies have concluded that the most productive years for the pastor may depend on longevity. Lyle Schaller found that the greatest growth of churches occurred in years five through eight of a pastor's tenure.[10] Kirk Hadaway, whose research was limited to Southern Baptist pastors, concluded that the most productive years were three through six.[11] And George Barna's data point to increasing productivity for pastors between years three and fifteen.[12]

A long-term pastorate neither guarantees growth nor promises productivity. More than a few pastors have become too comfortable in a long-term situation. But a short-term pastorate is almost always counterproductive. If over 90 percent of the churches in America best fit the description of a traditional church, the commitment to stay is vital. The vision to grow and to lead the church comes in small steps. Prayerful patience and persistent exhortation are requisites for deliberate change. For most traditional churches, large doses of major changes in a short period do a considerable amount of damage. The truly productive pastor of a traditional church will see his mission as long-term and count incremental steps as progress toward the goal.

Why are pastors less likely to remain in a church today? The answer can be seen from two perspectives. On the one hand, some churches have laity leadership that expects omnipotent performance by the pastor. If he does not meet all the unrealistic expectations of the people, he is considered expendable, even a burden. The CEO model dictates that if performance of the organization is inadequate, then the pastor must go so that a new scapegoat may be found.

I fear for churches and their leaders who take it upon themselves to determine God's call for a pastor. May God give us more people like one dear lady who told me that "she would not let me fail." She determined that her role in the church would be one of "praying for her pastor to succeed."

On the other hand, many pastors move from church to church for no other reason than to climb the ecclesiastical ladder. This numbers-crazed mentality sees bigger as better and mega as best. When discouragement or disillusionment comes into the pastor's life, he envisions his next church with a greener pasture and bigger flock.

When many pastors go through trials, difficulties, and criticisms in their churches, their first reaction is to move to another church. This is unfortunate because, quite often, the greatest promise is just on the other side of a great struggle.

Undoubtedly, God will call some pastors to move to another church after a short time. He is sovereign and knows best for the kingdom. It is difficult to believe, however, that the mobility we are seeing in American pastors today is good for our churches. If the traditional churches of our country are to make a difference for the kingdom, they will need leaders who will lead them through deliberate change over a long-term period. Are you committed to stay?

7. Do You Love Your Flock Unconditionally?

I once received a critical note from a church member. Unlike some of my peers in the ministry, I am a thin-skinned person who gets hurt easily by such comments. While I try to take such criticism in stride, the temptation to dwell on the negative is ever before me. In chapter 11 we will look in detail at this issue. For now, as pastor or other leader in your church, do you love the people of your church as Christ loves you? Sometimes we accept rather lightheartedly the unconditional love of Christ toward us. But we are to love others, even the most difficult of church members, with that same type of love. Do you love your flock unconditionally?

8. How Do You Look at Other Churches?

In my denomination, most of the 42,000 churches report a plethora of statistical data each year. It is not unusual, therefore, to see churches "ranked" by baptisms, new members, budget, and other factors. While such a numerical summary can be healthy if it engenders accountability and motivates leadership, it can be unhealthy if a competitive or jealous spirit develops among pastors.

This potential problem has grown in recent years with the enormous amount of publicity given to so-called "model churches." A model church is a fellowship that is recognized for notable achievements such as rapid numerical growth or innovative ministries. Such a church may be featured in magazines and books, or it could hold its own conferences in order that interested leaders could see the church firsthand. Certainly we can learn from these churches. The danger exists, however, when we feel inadequate compared to these model churches. How can our churches become a Willow Creek or Saddleback or Second Baptist, Houston? Or, on a more local level, why can we not baptize as many people as the sister church two miles away? Why did that church down the road draw fifty members from other local churches?

God desires to give you His vision for your church. But how can we keep our eyes on Him when we might be so preoccupied with the apparent success of other churches? Your faithfulness in ministry is not measured relative to other churches. Competitiveness among churches is nothing less than sinful disobedience. Do you rejoice at the growth of other churches? Are you praying for their pastors? How do you look at other churches?

9. How Do You Define Success?

The Church Growth Movement has taught us much in the past few decades.[13] It has shown us some of the sociological and organizational reasons for the growth or lack of growth in churches. The movement has also demonstrated the importance of numerical measurement as a method for accountability. I am very much in disagreement with the critics who insist that numbers and statistical information are out of place in the church. To the contrary, those churches that ignore their numerical realities are often the ones that demonstrate the lowest levels of responsibility and accountability. Numbers can be healthy if used in a proper context and with the right motive.

On the other hand, I hear the concern of the critics who are concerned that numbers may become the end instead of the means for churches. While we must be ever conscious of growth rates, attendance levels, conversions, and other numerically measurable concerns, we cannot let such numbers be our ultimate measures for success. True success is nothing more and nothing less than obedience to God. Results, numerical and otherwise, will usually be positive if we are obedient. But even if they are not positive, we will be deemed successful to God if we are faithful. How do you define success?

10. Do You Have an Attitude of Gratitude?

One of my sons showed me a poem in one of his textbooks. The primary character in the poem was a wise man who was approached by two strangers. The first stranger, a newcomer to the city, asked the wise man what kind of people lived in the city. The wise man responded with a question: "What kind of people live in the town from where you came?" The first stranger then described his fellow citizens as mean-spirited, untrustworthy, and self-centered. The wise man responded, "You will find the people very much like that here."

The second stranger, who arrived later, asked the identical question, with the wise man responding with the same question. But this time the second stranger said that his fellow citizens were kind, trustworthy, and concerned for others. The wise man once again responded, "You will find the people very much like that here."

The manner in which we lead our churches, communicate God's vision, and encourage enthusiasm will be directly related to our attitude toward the church and the people. If we focus on the negative, the critical people, and the unpleasant tasks, we will see our churches as the first stranger viewed his hometown. But we can choose God's way of being thankful and joyous at the abundance of blessings He has given us. Paul wrote to the Philippian church: "Finally, brothers, whatever is true, whatever is noble, whatever is right, whatever is pure, whatever is admirable—if anything is excellent or praiseworthy—think about such things" (Phil. 4:8).

Sometimes it takes a rude awakening for us pastors to realize how blessed we are. I was in the middle of a pity party about some difficult church matters when the telephone rang. The friend who called me was asking for prayers. He had just been fired from his job; he and his family of four did not know where to turn. The incident reminded me of the old saying: "I cried because I had no shoes until I met a man who had no feet."

Pastors, church leaders—are you thanking God every day for his mercy, blessings, and love? Are you focusing on the good, instead of dwelling on the negative? Do you have an attitude of gratitude?

Now . . . the Next Step

Leading a traditional church can be a most rewarding experience if the leadership begins with God. Some of the questions I asked may have been just for you. In the next three chapters we will travel step by step in the process of discovering, communicating, and implementing God's vision in your church. But this first chapter had to be written. Unless God's leaders are right with our Lord, we cannot expect blessings and followship.

None of what you will read is an easy solution. Indeed a mad rush to implement most of the principles may result in discord, fear, and factions in your church. Go at God's pace. Eat the elephant one bite at a time. But please do not stand still. Too much is at stake to do nothing.

And remember, church growth begins with God. Your dependence on Him may prove to be the difference between stagnation and revival. In that regard, I would like to leave you with one of my favorite poems. I wish I knew the author. This simple piece of poetry speaks volumes about a person who learned true dependence on the Savior.

The Road of Life

At first, I saw God as my observer,
my judge,
keeping track of the things I did wrong,
so as to know whether I merited heaven
or hell when I die.
He was out there sort of like a president.
I recognized his picture when I saw it,
but I really didn't know him.

But later on
when I met Christ,
it seemed as though life were rather like a bike ride,
but it was a tandem bike,
and I noticed that Christ
was in the back helping me pedal.

I don't know just when it was
that he suggested we change places,
but life has not been the same since.

When I had control.
I knew the way.
It was rather boring,
but predictable . . .
It was the shortest distance between two points.

But when he took the lead,
He knew delightful long cuts,
up mountains,
and through rocky places
at breakneck speeds,
it was all I could do to hang on!
Even though it looked like madness,
He said, "Pedal!"

I worried and was anxious
and asked,
"Where are you taking me?"
He laughed and didn't answer,
and I started to learn to trust.

I forgot my boring life
and entered into the adventure.
And when I'd say, "I'm scared,"
he'd lean back and touch my hand.

He took me to people with gifts that I needed,
gifts of healing,
acceptance
and joy.
They gave me gifts to take on my journey,
my Lord's and mine.

And we were off again.
He said, "Give the gifts away;
They're extra baggage, too much weight."
So I did,
to the people we met,
and I found that in giving I received,
and still our burden was light.
I did not trust him
at first,
in control of my life.
I thought he'd wreck it;
but he knows bike secrets,
knows how to make it bend to take sharp corners,
knows how to jump to clear high rocks,
knows how to fly to shorten scary passages.

And I am learning to shut up
and pedal
in the strangest places,
and I'm beginning to enjoy the view
and the cool breeze on my face
with my delightful constant companion, Jesus Christ.
And when I'm sure I just can't do anymore,
He just smiles and says . . . "Pedal."

                                        -- author unknown

Pedal on! The best is yet to come!

NOTES

1. For a more detailed discussion of the purpose of the church, see my book: Thom S. Rainer, *The Book of Church Growth: History, Theology, and Principles* (Nashville: Broadman, 1993), 147-58.

2. C. Peter Wagner, *Your Church Can Be Healthy* (Nashville: Abingdon, 1979), 87.

3. George Barna, *Today's Pastors* (Ventura, Calif: Regal, 1993), 32.

4. Ibid.

5. Ibid.

6. Ibid., 38.

7. Ibid.

8. C. Kirk Hadaway, *Church Growth Principles: Separating Fact from Fiction* (Nashville: Broadman, 1991), 164, emphasis added.

9. Barna, 36.

10. Lyle Schaller, *Growing Plans* (Nashville: Abingdon, 1975), 96.

11. Hadaway, 77.

12. Barna, 37.

13. See Rainer, *The Book of Church Growth,* for a comprehensive history of the Church Growth Movement.

CHAPTER 2

REKINDLING THE VISION IN A TRADITIONAL CHURCH

"Your young men will see visions,
your old men will dream dreams."
Acts 2:17

St. Petersburg, Florida, was a great place to live! The years I served as a pastor there are counted among my fondest memories. Perhaps the climate had a lot to do with my love of the city. With only rare exceptions, St. Petersburg had two seasons: warm and hot. My boys and I would walk in the yard in our bare feet year-round. I particularly remember one Christmas day after the boys had opened their gifts. I asked them if they had anything particular they would like to do for the remainder of the day. My middle son, Art, made the suggestion that we go to the beach. And we did! To this day, my family still talks about Christmas at the beach.

About the only thing I missed in St. Petersburg was a fireplace. When we moved to Alabama, the Rainer family was delighted to find and purchase a home with a fireplace. The warmth and coziness of a mid-winter fire engendered feelings of security and closeness. But the fire would eventually die without more wood and occasional stoking. The bright blaze would become nothing more than flickering embers.

Many traditional churches are like the flames in the fireplace. When they began the fire burned bright; the vision was clear. Years later, only faint flickers provide reminders of the way it used to be and, more importantly, the way it could be. A rekindled vision is needed desperately for the church to carry out its mission.

A Tale of Two Pastors

Into this scenario comes the pastor of the church. His leadership, priorities, and the decisions he makes will have a lot to say about the future of the church. How will he respond?

In the many churches with which I have had the privilege to consult and to do conferences, I have noticed that pastors in these traditional churches have a tendency to exhibit one of two patterns of behavior. While I have never known a pastor who demonstrates the extreme behaviors of the following two fictitious men, I have known some who are close!

Pastor Bulldozer

After only four months at Christ Community Church, Pastor Bulldozer had created more problems than anyone could remember in the church's fifty-three-year history. In the first few weeks the church members accepted Pastor Bulldozer's aggressive personality. After all, the church had given a mandate to the pastor search committee to find a man whose strong leadership skills could move the church off its numerical plateau. For over fifteen years, the church's attendance had remained at virtually the same level. Occasional gains would quickly be offset by losses.

But the church never expected a person like Pastor Bulldozer! His first Sunday in the pulpit he announced that all decision-making authority would be transferred to him. The committees, the constitution and by-laws, and the business meetings, he stated, were "bureaucratic nightmares" that hindered God's work at Christ Church.

At the end of his first month at the church, he told the workers in a Sunday School meeting that everyone involved in Sunday School "must be involved in outreach visitation at least ten weeks per quarter." Furthermore, the workers would give their outreach report forms to him, where he would keep track of all the contacts and visits. Anyone who did not participate would be asked to leave their Sunday School position.

While these two issues caused ongoing murmuring, the coup de grace occurred in the fourth month of the new pastor's ministry. When the church gathered for the 11:00 A.M. worship service on that crisp October morning, the change was evident immediately. The treasured third-generational hymnbooks had been replaced by new books replete

36

with contemporary hymns. The pastor mentioned the change briefly in that morning service, mumbling something about "the old fossils had finally been removed."

Pastor Bulldozer's five-month tenure at Christ Church was the shortest in the church's history.

Pastor Passive

The celebration was like none Wagnerstown Baptist had seen in half a century. The occasion of Pastor Passive's fifteenth anniversary had been planned to a minute detail by the hospitality committee. The building and grounds committee had worked weeks to get the facilities and landscaping in good shape. And the finance committee, working jointly with the promotion committee, arranged for the big gift for Pastor and Mrs. Passive.

After a day of meals, singing, and testimonies, the presentation was made. Mr. Browning, chairman of the deacons, gave the honored couple keys to a new and shiny minivan. Tears, hugs, and appreciation flowed both ways. Shortly thereafter the celebration ended and the participants returned to their homes.

Pastor Passive had difficulty sleeping that night. The past fifteen years played like a fast-forwarded movie before his mind's eye. He had come to the church with a mandate for change from the search committee. Wagnerstown Baptist, once the premier growth church in Wagnerstown, had seen a steady erosion in numerical membership for over a decade. The young and excited Pastor Passive seemed to be the answer to the church's dilemma.

The pastor's first year had seen some healthy results. Prospects became members as he led a new emphasis on outreach and evangelism. The honeymoon period was a time of excitement and modest growth.

The first signs of trouble come in the second year. The issue was a new Sunday School class started and taught by Ken McMillan, a new veterinarian in town. His popular class had drawn a few members from established classes. Complaints trickled in to the pastor about this new man hurting their fellowship.

And then there was the situation with Buddy King, the astute owner and manager of the newly started sign-painting company. His nomination to the finance committee seemed at the time a prudent move. After all, Wagnerstown Baptist needed at least token representation from the "outsiders" in the church. But Buddy's suggestions for improved financial record-keeping and cost-saving innovations ran counter to the ideas of the rest of the committee. Though Buddy's recommendations were clearly in the best interest of the church, the response was consistent: "We've never done it that way before."

Two separate meetings were placed on Pastor Passive's calendar as a result of the finance committee fiasco. The first meeting was with Richard Williams, finance committee chairman. He warned the pastor of some of the problems with the "new folks" who "just did not understand the way we did things." A subtle threat was added about the "big givers" in the church. Pastor Passive assured Mr. Williams that he would take care of matters.

The second meeting was with Buddy King. The new member mentioned his initial excitement about Wagnerstown Baptist, an excitement that was rapidly waning. He presented his finance proposals to the pastor. Though Pastor Passive saw their merit, he suggested that they "leave well-enough alone." Buddy King and his family soon left the church.

Other conflicts arose, the fifteen-year pastor recalled from his bed that night. He did not remember a specific time that he decided to avoid conflict. It just happened. He started putting all of his energies into home and hospital visitation to the members. He kept them very happy with this attention. So diligent was the pastor that even the deacons saw no need for hospital visitation since they knew that Pastor Passive would be there daily. The conflict diminished and the church stopped growing. Fifteen years later the average attendance was 160, compared to 157 at the beginning of the pastor's ministry.

Seeing Visions, Dreaming Dreams

Neither Pastor Bulldozer nor Pastor Passive had a healthy approach to leading their traditional churches to growth. Both saw a massive undertaking. One tried to tackle the entire project in a few months. The other saw such a large obstacle that he ignored it altogether.

In order to understand the task at hand, we can look at a visual representation of a healthy church. Such a church goes through continuous cycles of rekindling the vision so that real ministry can take place.

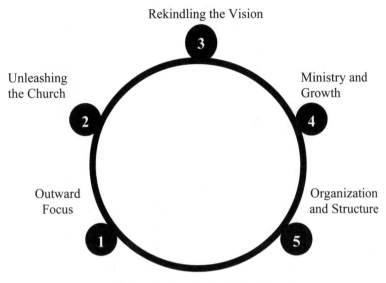

Rekindling the Vision

3

Unleashing
the Church

Ministry and
Growth

2

4

Outward
Focus

Organization
and Structure

1

5

Vision Cycle of a Healthy Church

Vision Cycle of a Healthy Traditional Church

We church growth enthusiasts often use the example of the Jerusalem church to describe the dynamic process of vision discovery and implementation. We turn to Acts 2:17 as our prooftext that the people must be given a vision for ministry. I believe, however, that we have made two major mistakes in utilizing this passage. First, we assume that the vision must precede all meaningful ministry. Second, we at least imply that vision discovery is a "top-down" process (i.e. it flows from God to the pastor to the people).

It would seem that the vision for the Jerusalem church was preceded by three years of instruction by Jesus. He reminded His followers that their mission was to have an outward focus (cf. Matt. 10:7 ff.); that they were to be a "going" church (28:18-20); and that the "going" would have no geographical boundaries (Acts 1:8). Before the vision there came a change in mind-set: the church would look outward.

A second fallacy in much of the literature about vision today is that the pastor must somehow get a direct word from God about the vision, communicate it to the church, and get the people to "own" the vision. The biblical reality is that God desires to speak to all of the people of the church about vision. The very nature of spiritual gifts is that they are God's way of showing each believer's purpose (vision) in the larger vision of the church. The pastor who unilaterally determines the vision of the church without any awareness of the spiritual giftedness and passions of the people is headed for trouble. He may have a game plan with no players. The wise "coach" develops his strategy for the "team" according to the "talent" already present.

Understanding the Cycle in Your Church

Let us return to the cycle illustration to understand how the process might work in your church. It must be understood that the healthy church is ever moving along the cycle. Unhealthy churches remain fixed at one point on the cycle.

Organization and Structure. It is not uncommon to find a traditional church resting on this point of the cycle. The church in its past began looking outward. The people became excited as they realized that they were a vital part of this plan. A vision began to develop as ministry and missions unfolded in the church. The church eventually had many different organizations and structures to carry forth the vision and ministries of the church.

For many churches, the organizations and structure become an end instead of a means. Originally conceived to carry out the vision, they now exist because "we've always done it that way." Like the island farmers described in the previous chapter, the practice exists for no known reason. Members become attached to and nostalgic about the structure. Rather than speak further about this point on the cycle, the next chapter will be devoted to this single issue. Such a lengthy discussion is necessary since many, perhaps a majority of, traditional churches remain fixed and entrenched here.

Outward Focus. Moving from entrenched structures to vital ministries requires not a specific vision at this point, but a new mindset. The church must move from an inward focus to an outward focus. I once consulted with a church that needed many obvious changes in the physical structure of their buildings. A patient building committee listened to concerns about changing a structure that had become extremely comfortable to many of the people.

When I was asked to speak to the church, I shared with them the building I saw as an outsider. I attempted to explain how I would view the preschool facilities, the worship center, and the restrooms as a lost or unchurched person. And then I said: "You folks need to decide if the purpose of the building is to keep you comfortable or to reach beyond your walls." That one sentence seemed to make the difference. The church moved from organizational and structural entrenchment to a new outward focus.

Your first step in rekindling the vision in a traditional church may simply be a redirection of energies from maintenance to outreach. In one of the most exhaustive studies of church and denominational growth in decades, an outward focus was deemed to be one of the most important factors in leading a church to growth. Indeed the relationship between an outward focus and growth was stronger than previously estimated.[1] We will look at a proposed plan of action for your church at the conclusion of this chapter.

Unleashing the Church. A church must move from the stage of outward focus to the next stage if it is to move from ideas to action. The next step could be called "the permission stage." Many Christians simply do not think they can fulfill their calling and giftedness in a traditional church. In many cases they may be right! The mind-set may be that the leadership (staff, denomination, etc.) is responsible for creating ministries and programs, and that the people will be expected to participate in them. And participation in a particular ministry by a church member may have no relationship to his or her giftedness.

This stage in the cycle of a traditional church is more informational and equipping than actual ministry. It involves the communication of "permission" to do ministry beyond the existing ministry structures.

It is at this point on the cycle that the church must help the people of the church discover (and rediscover) their spiritual gifts. Many of the active members in our churches have been through one or more spiritual gift seminars. Redundancy, however, is important. The people must understand that meaningful ministry takes place when they are exercising their spiritual gifts.

Equally important to such teaching devices on spiritual gifts as seminars, classes, and videos is the actual opportunity for individuals to take tests or inventories that guide them toward spiritual gift discovery.

The key in successfully utilizing these inventories is threefold. First, they must be taken by as many of the adult church members as possible. An initial seminar may include 10 to 30 percent of the membership. The church might set a goal of testing three-fourths of the adult resident membership within a three-year period. That would be followed by persistent follow up on the members who have not taken the inventory and a request or requirement that all new members participate in the process.

Second, a key individual in the church must be responsible for the entire spiritual gifts ministry. The administrative responsibility is not overwhelming, but its success will depend on a leader for the ministry.

Finally, these inventories must be really utilized. They are not to sit in a file or box gathering dust. Ministry placement decisions should be very much contingent upon a person's spiritual gifts.

The key purpose of this step in the cycle, unleashing the church, is to create first an awareness and then a burden for the people to do ministry. It may be a slow process as the church members rethink ministry. For many of them, doing ministry has been limited to filling a vacancy on a committee or in Sunday School. The full realization that they have permission to start and lead ministries may come slowly. And leaders in existing organizations and structures may feel threatened by these changes. Proceed prayerfully, deliberately, and purposefully.

Rekindling the Vision. While it may seem unusual to discuss the vision at this point of the cycle, it is vital that the two previous steps precede vision discovery. The church is now looking outward, and, individually, many of the members are considering their giftedness and contribution to the body.

Only when the members begin to express their individual giftedness and callings can a pastor truly begin to assess the direction God is leading the church. For example, at a church I pastored, we had proceeded through the outward-focus stage and the unleashing-the-church stage. Many individuals in the church began expressing their desire to utilize their gifts in ministries, some of which did not previously exist in the church. For me as pastor, discovering the vision of the church was no complex or mystical procedure. I simply saw how God was leading the people. Two significant patterns had developed. A substantial number of members had expressed desires to use their gifts to strengthen the family. Another group saw themselves a missionaries, evangelists, teachers, and administrators in new church works. Two key components of the church's vision thus became strengthening the family and starting new churches. The people of the church were ready, prepared, and excited to move in this direction.

Such a "bottom-up" vision discovery seems to make more biblical sense than a mandated vision from the pastor. Of course the pastor must have the God-given wisdom to discern such a movement from God and then to communicate it to the church. But the vision truly begins with the people.

Ministry and Growth. This stage of the vision is perhaps the most exciting for the church. No longer is the church mired in an organizational and structural rut. A renewed outreach emphasis and the discovery of the church's vision through the unleashed people result in ministry and growth. The church is making a difference for the kingdom. Lives are being changed and people are being won to Christ.

How long did it take to get the church to this point? The answer really varies with each church, but rare is the traditional church that can circle the vision cycle in a year or two. Indeed, the process of moving from an inward organizational focus to an outward focus may itself take one or two years. Rekindling the vision which results in real ministry and growth may not occur for five or more years. Perhaps this sluggishness is at least a partial explanation for the observation that a pastor's most effective years of ministry begin at some point past the fifth year. Are you willing to take the deliberate but steady pace toward ministry and growth? Will you be content with three steps forward and two steps backward? And will you continue to lead your church along the vision cycle even when you encounter obstacles?

Perhaps the most difficult aspect of answering these questions has to do with the role of the pastor. If you are the pastor of a traditional church, will you be willing to make the slow transition from doing the ministry to equipping others for ministry (Eph. 4:11-13)? While you certainly will not abandon your shepherding calling, will you equip others to share this ministry with you? Will you be able to say "no" to some of the frivolous requests that are made of you? Will you acknowledge that your first responsibility of ministry is to your family (1 Tim. 3:5)? Will you focus your time and energies on the ministry of the Word and on prayer (Acts 6:4)? This stage of ministry and growth must include the pastor's willingness to become a biblically defined pastor.

Organization and Structure. This stage of the vision cycle is often perceived negatively by visionary leaders. After all, the organization and structure can be an obstacle to future growth and ministry. However, this stage is a vital part of the vision cycle. The ministry and growth cannot be sustained in chaos. Structure is a healthy and necessary next step.

In Paul's early letters to the churches, his words often exude the enthusiasm of one who was testifying about churches in the ministry and growth stage (Eph. 1:15; Phil. 1:3-6; 2 Thess. 1:30). But by the time he wrote the later-dated pastoral letters, Paul expressed his concern for order and organization in worship (1 Tim. 2:1-15); church structure (3:1-13); ministry (5:1-21); and doctrine (Titus 2:1-15).

It is not the organization and structure per se that is an obstacle to ministry and growth. The problem occurs when the purpose of the structure is no longer relevant. Does it exist to carry forth the vision of the church? Or has its purpose long since outlived its usefulness? Does it exist for reasons of nostalgia and fear of change? If so, the church must renew its outward focus, which brings us full circle in the vision cycle.

Plan of Action: An Example

The final portion of this chapter will offer a plan of action for a traditional church to move along the vision cycle. It is written with the understanding that, without practical application, the vision cycle may prove to be no more than theoretical confusion. The danger in providing practical examples, however, is that church leaders may

44

apply the proposal in detail, without considering what works best in their own context. The following information, therefore, is given as an example, not a proposal.

From Organizational Entrenchment to Outward Focus

A church that has become stale organizationally, more concerned about procedures than evangelism, and argumentative about the most insignificant items needs a new focus. The church has ceased to be the church because its concern is institutional maintenance or survival. The people of the church have become spiritual navel gazers. They cannot see beyond themselves or their church in its status quo state.

A pastor's natural response to such a condition is to attack the structure. Such a move may be the pastor's greatest mistake. I have known pastors who have had great concerns about constitutions and by-laws which hinder effective ministry. A common response has been to change the structure, a document in this case. But the document is not the problem. The need is to change attitudes rather than structure. In fact, the church will need to go full circle on the vision cycle before structural changes should be made.

How can we turn hearts from inward to outward? It begins by directing the church's resources and energies beyond its walls. The outreach visitation night, for example, may be ineffective and poorly attended. A monthly meal and major emphasis may bring life back into the outreach ministry. The ongoing outreach can be managed within the Sunday School classes.

Regular emphases to discover community needs, perhaps once a month as well, can rekindle fires of outreach. The community survey we used at several churches has proved to be a very effective and non-threatening tool. The steps we used are as follows:

1. We knock on a door and ask the person to complete the survey after we leave.
2. Before leaving we state that the purpose of our survey is to meet community needs.
3. The resident completes the survey and leaves it on their doorknob. (The survey has a perforated top that enables it to be hung in this fashion.)

4. We return to pick up the survey within an hour, without further disturbing the resident.
5. If the resident requested any information or activities, we follow up at an appropriate time.
6. We send a thank-you note to everyone who responded.

THANK YOU ...

... for taking the time to complete this simple information card. When you have completed the information, please place this card on your door, and we will return within the hour and pick it up.

Family Name _____

Address _____

Phone _____ Zip _____

Person completing this form_____

FAMILY MEMBERS

	Name	Age
Head of House	_____	_____
Spouse	_____	_____
Children	_____	_____
	_____	_____
	_____	_____
	_____	_____

What do you think is the greatest need in our area?

Why do you think most people do not attend church?

(over)

If you were looking for a church, what kind of things would you look for?

Please check any activities you would like to see offered to meet the needs of our area:
_____ Home Bible Studies
_____ Aerobics/Fitness Classes
_____ Saturday Evening Worship Services
_____ Sporting Activities
_____ Topical Studies
_____ Summer Christian Education for Children
_____ Mother's Day Out
_____ Marriage Enrichment Seminars
_____ Single Parents Ministry
_____ Parent's Night Out
_____ Youth Activities
_____ Financial Planning
_____ Big Brother/Big Sister

Others:

I'd like more information on:
_____ How to Become a Christian
_____ Adult Bible Studies
_____ Children's Bible Studies
_____ Singles Activities
_____ Youth Activities
_____ Spiritual Growth
_____ Please Place Me on Your Mail-Out

We at _____ Church care about you and our community. Would you let us know how we can help you?

Comments, Requests, or Prayer Needs:

Moving Toward an Unleashed Church

The outward focus moves a church from an institutional mindset to an outreach and ministry mindset. Eventually, however, the new outward focus must move from general principles to specific application in the lives of the church members. How can your church best make this transition? Perhaps the following example can be adopted to your situation.

1. Preach, teach, write, and emphasize laity ministry. Remind your people in as many opportunities as possible that they are the ministers of the church (Eph. 4:12). Recognize laity ministry in your morning services. Emphasize that these ministries began as a burden in the hearts of the people, not the pastor or other staff. Preach messages from Acts and Paul's letters where the emphasis is on the work of ministry by the people.

2. Pray that God will lead you to find a leader for spiritual gifts ministry. One layperson in the church sold on the biblical precept of spiritual gifts can be an instrument of revival. That person can organize an initial spiritual gifts seminar. The purpose of such a seminar is to instruct on spiritual gifts and to lead the people toward the discovery of their own spiritual gifts. Spiritual gift inventories can be taken and interpreted.

Unfortunately, many churches have a single emphasis on spiritual gifts and then move to other areas. Like the Sunday School organization, spiritual gifts ministry must be ongoing. Such is the reason that a leader is so vitally needed. He or she can lead future seminars; work one-on-one with people who have not gone through the seminars and inventories; see that all new members are spiritual gift-assessed; and, most importantly, keep this information available for consideration for ministry positions.

It is a revival-like spirit that occurs when ministry positions are filled according to giftedness instead of more arbitrary factors. Ministry for the people becomes a joy instead of a burden. Recruitment based on gifts is fun and exciting. (Imagine that in a traditional church!) The body of Christ, your local church, begins to have a biblical look about it (1 Cor. 12).

3. Take ministry risks. As the ministry mind-set permeates the church, individuals will begin to see a light that tells them: "I can do ministry that's not even a part of the church programs!" Those individuals will come to you and ask you for permission to start and lead a new ministry. How will you respond? My experience has been that it's better to err on the side of permission rather than denial. While a few ideas for ministry may be obvious duds, the greater number will be truly God-sent. Though our temptation as leaders might be to oversee and lead the new ministry, we must leave them in the hands of God and the persons to whom He has spoken. The apostle Paul experienced the same struggle when he was seeking God's direction on whether or not to leave a church on its own. His final decision would be: "with prayer and fasting, [he] committed them to the Lord in whom they had put their trust" (Acts 12:5). And so must we.

Rekindling the Vision: A "People-Led" Discovery

The plethora of information I received about churches needing a vision made sense to me. I was in my first full-time pastorate, and the church sorely needed a clear direction. But I must confess that I was uncomfortable with the "pastor-led" model of vision: God speaks to pastor; pastor informs and leads people. The model can be illustrated as follows:

God
VISION

Pastor/Leader
VISION

People of the Church

PASTOR-LED VISION MODEL

48

If the Holy Spirit truly speaks to Christians without the need of an earthly priest, and if spiritual gifts come directly from the Holy Spirit to Christians, then something seems askew about the pastor-led model. It would seem that the New Testament pattern would be one where God, through the giving of spiritual gifts and through His speaking to individuals about their call to ministry, would begin with the entire body rather than with a lone individual. This people-led model looks different from the pastor-led model:

God

MINISTRY   **SPIRITUAL**
CALLING   **GIFTS**

People of the Church

Ministry according to Giftedness and Calling

VISION

Pastor discerns and communicates vision according to the giftedness and ministry of the people.

PEOPLE-LED VISION MODEL

The pastor's role in this model is to discern what God is already doing in the church, communicate that vision to the people, and equip

49

the people as they continue to develop ministries according to the vision. I was amazed at churches where we continued to see ministries for families and new churches grow naturally. God spoke to the people and gave me the wisdom to discern His work.

A possible objection to this vision model is that it weakens the leadership role of the pastor. I would disagree strongly! Remember, on the vision cycle, the pastor leads the church past organizational entrenchment to an outward focus. He then leads in the refinement of the outward focus to particular callings and giftedness. Next he discerns God's work and vision according to the ministries that have unfolded. He begins communications and rekindles the vision, while continuing to equip those in ministry. Strong leadership skills are a must to move this far on the vision cycle!

At least one possible exception to this model should be noted. In a new church it is not unusual for the vision to come directly from God to the founding pastor. In this situation the pastor is really "the people." Those who come to the new church will be the people whose giftedness best fit the vision of the new church.

But in a traditional church the people are already in place. The pastor (except the founding pastor) arrives later. His role is to discover the calls and gifts of the body of Christ and to lead that local fellowship toward understanding and fulfilling the vision God has given it.

Ministry and Growth: A Natural Step

Church growth and ministry is a natural process. It should happen in traditional churches. What the pastor and leaders of the church have done to this point is to remove those obstacles that hinder growth and ministry. Those obstacles included: an inward focus, organizational entrenchment, mismatched gifts with ministry, and an uncertain purpose.

The analogy to plant growth is appropriate here. The plant is watered, put into the sunlight, provided proper nutrients, and kept at a growth-inducive temperature. Such efforts may have included some human efforts, but the plant grows. It is a natural process that cannot be achieved by human effort.

God, in His gracious and loving way, allows us to colabor with Him in preparing the church for growth. But this next step is His and His alone. The church grows and ministry takes place. It is natural, and it is God's plan. "What after all, is Apollos? And what is Paul? Only servants, through whom you came to believe—as the Lord has assigned to each his task. I planted the seed, Apollos watered it, but God made it grow" (1 Cor. 3:5-6).

The Necessity of Organization and Structure

Earlier in this chapter it was mentioned that some church leaders see stale organizations and structures as the primary problem in the church and, thus, attack the structure. The vision cycle shows that such action is premature and perhaps unhealthy for the church. The church must proceed through four other steps on the cycle before changing the organizational structure.

For example, the deacon leadership in a church I served saw the need to change the way they do ministry. For years they had attempted to carry out a deacon family ministry, where each deacon has pastoral ministry responsibility for a group of families. We discovered that those deacons with shepherding gifts enjoyed the ministry and were very effective in their work. But deacons who had different interests, gifts, and desires placed the family ministry low on their list of priorities. They felt guilty for doing so.

The deacon chairman took a bold step and suggested that the deacons do their servant-ministry by spiritual gifts. The response was exciting! The different ministry teams that were started by the deacons include: evangelism; new members; inactive members; widows and senior adults; crisis ministry; and, of course, family ministry.

Accountability forms were maintained. Meetings of the teams became a regular occurrence. The structure developed after the other stages on the vision cycle had been completed. The previous structure, the deacon family ministry plan, was greatly modified with this new approach to ministry. However, the change in the structure followed a new outward focus, spiritual gifts emphasis, and a rekindled vision.

Putting It All Together: A Vision Rekindled

Does your church need a new enthusiasm, a new direction, and a rekindled vision? With God's power, your church can become a revitalized force for the kingdom. Meaningless programs and dying organizations can give way to meaningful ministry and dynamic outward focus. Let us see the vision cycle with some of the examples previously mentioned.

As you lead your church in a step-by-step process that may be similar to this vision cycle, learn to wait—both on God and your people. Be patient as you move one step at a time. Never doubt the power of prayer as you listen to the voice of God directing your next move. Different churches will move at different paces, but I am convinced God will honor your desire to rekindle His vision in your churches.

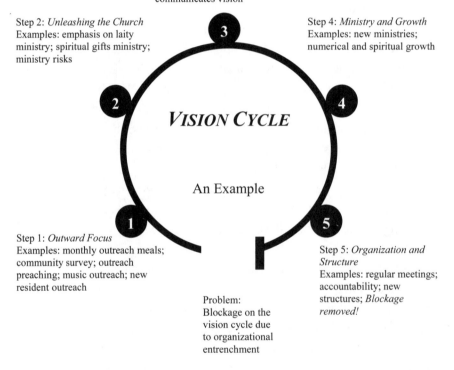

Step 3: *Rekindling the Vision*
Examples: people-led vision; pastor communicates vision

Step 2: *Unleashing the Church*
Examples: emphasis on laity ministry; spiritual gifts ministry; ministry risks

Step 4: *Ministry and Growth*
Examples: new ministries; numerical and spiritual growth

VISION CYCLE

An Example

Step 1: *Outward Focus*
Examples: monthly outreach meals; community survey; outreach preaching; music outreach; new resident outreach

Step 5: *Organization and Structure*
Examples: regular meetings; accountability; new structures; *Blockage removed!*

Problem:
Blockage on the vision cycle due to organizational entrenchment

NOTES

1. This outstanding study is: David A. Roozen and C. Kirk Hadaway, eds., *Church and Denominational Growth* (Nashville: Abingdon, 1993). The specific chapter to which I refer here is C. Kirk Hadaway, "Is Evangelistic Activity Related to Church Growth?", 169 - 87.

CHAPTER 3

GETTING OUT OF THE RUT

"For God so loved the world
that he didn't send a committee."
Hezekiah 3:16

When I was a teenager, my hometown had several dirt roads. While paved roads were available between most points, the dirt roads often offered the shortest path and the greatest adventure. By the time I got my driver's license I was on my way with friends on some of the most wicked roads!

During dry weather we would travel in ruts in the road that had been created by cars driving in the same paths day after day. Those ruts would be a challenge because they often were deep enough to control the direction of the car. But the real challenge would come during or soon after a rain. The top layer of dirt in the ruts would be loose from the constant travel of cars over it. After a good rainstorm, that layer of dirt could turn into a mud trap for the unsuspecting traveler.

I do not know how many times I got stuck in a rut in a south Alabama red, dirt road. My friends and I would push from the rear while one person steered the car. On several occasions our efforts were unsuccessful. We would take the long walking journey to the nearest telephone to ask someone to get us out of the rut.

You may feel like your church is in a rut. One dictionary offers two definitions for "rut." The first meaning says "a furrow or track in the ground, especially one made by the passage of a vehicle or vehicles." The second definition is "a fixed and dull or unpromising way of life." Both ruts are caused by routine and repetition. And both ruts can stop forward progress. If you have ever been in a car stuck in the mud, you know that you can press the accelerator and the tires will spin. But that activity will only put you deeper in the rut. Forward motion ceases.

The purpose of this chapter is to address the "rut issue." Many traditional churches do a lot of things; indeed activity (meetings, programs, full calendars) is a way of life. But the activity is often like the car spinning in the mud. No significant forward progress is evident.

Back to the Vision Cycle

Let us return to the vision cycle for a moment. Remember, the idea behind the cycle is one of continuous movement. A church will begin to leave the point of organizational entrenchment when it has an outward focus. As the people of the church are given permission to do ministry, they discover their spiritual gifts and passions. The Holy Spirit makes clear the direction and vision of the church from the way He directs His people. The vision is clarified and communicated, and real growth and ministry result. Soon this new growth and ministry will take on a structure and become organized.

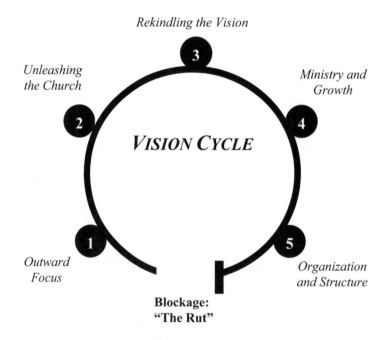

Rekindling the Vision

3

Unleashing the Church

Ministry and Growth

2

VISION CYCLE

4

1

5

Outward Focus

Organization and Structure

Blockage: "The Rut"

BLOCKAGE OF THE VISION CYCLE

The problem often occurs in a traditional church when the church stops on the vision cycle at the point of organization and structure. This is depicted on the vision cycle as "the rut." Ideally, the church would move beyond its organization with a continued outward focus, which would eventually bring it back full circle with new and fresh organizations and structures.

Why is this point of the vision cycle the place where churches often stagnate? In the third section of this book we will look at specific attitudes that develop when a church stops in the rut of the vision cycle. For now let us examine some reasons why many churches fail to move beyond the organization and structure point of the vision cycle.

Reasons for the Rut

Second Faith Church of Delongsville, Colorado, had a glorious twenty-year history. It began as a mission of First Faith Church with a group of people who were dedicated to missions and evangelism. The core group of thirty-five developed a coordinated and exciting outreach ministry that led the church to grow to two hundred members by their fifth year. The long-range plan for the church called for the purchase of land by the fifth year and a detailed building program for years six through fifteen.

With precision the church saw most of its original dreams and goals fulfilled. One year before the planned fifteenth year, the church moved into its new worship center. Second Faith accounted for five hundred members and almost three hundred in average attendance its fifteenth year. The church was enjoying a new worship center, a four-year old fellowship hall, and relatively new education facilities. With the luxury of new buildings the people continued the outreach ministry of their original dream. The potential for growth and ministry seemed unlimited.

But by the time the church celebrated its twentieth anniversary the excitement had diminished. Though some new members were joining the church, the growth barely offset the losses. Second Faith's motto, "The Church with a Vision," sounded like a cruel joke to those who had known better days.

What happened between years fifteen and twenty? Why did a church with such a fantastic beginning see their momentum come to a stop in just a few, short years? Second Faith had traveled one loop along the vision cycle. They began with an outward focus and people who were passionate and gifted for outreach. The vision to reach the community became clearer and clearer. Growth and ministry seemed to happen naturally.

Prior to the fifteenth year, however, the church saw their visions and dreams become organized and structured. New buildings were built to accommodate the growth. The innovative outreach ministry became a major program of the church. This organization and structure point on the vision cycle represented the first full cycle in the history of the church. The buildings and programs became the symbols of the church's successes. No one asked the question, "Where do we go from here?" Second Faith Church was in a rut for at least five reasons. And these reasons are common to many traditional churches whose best days seem to be in the past.

1. Success

Success is a primary reason that churches get into a rut. A completed building program is often the culmination of years of growth. The new facility is a structure to house the people who were attracted to the vision, ministry, and growth of the church. That new building is seen as the reward for and fruition of years of prayer and labor rather than the new people and changed lives that motivated the church to build. The changed lives and new members who necessitated the new building are forgotten. The facility becomes an end rather than a means. The monument that was supposed to be a symbol of the blessings of God is now an idol that receives more attention than people in need. The building is not inherently evil, but the attitude of the people toward the building is misplaced and sinful. For the church to listen clearly to the voice of God, it must look beyond the structure to a new outward focus.

Perhaps you are familiar with a church that has become legalistic with its constitution and by-laws. The original intent of the documents was to bring order and organization to a positive situation. But now the document has become an end instead of a means. Ministry and needed change cannot take place without peeling back layers of bureaucracy. As one staff member told me in a church I consulted: "We've stopped trying to be innovative and attentive to the Spirit's leading. It's too much trouble and pain to change anything around here."

2. Routine

I almost always sleep on the same side of the bed every night. The habit began early in my marriage when Jo and I could afford only one bedside lamp. In an attempt to be a gentleman, I offered Jo the side of the bed with the lamp. I would read with less light. (I know my sacrifice overwhelms you!)

It has been several years since we had only one lamp. But guess what? I still sleep on the same side of the bed. Like most other people, I am a creature of habit.

Second Faith Church developed an innovative outreach ministry early in its history. After several years the ministry was fine-tuned into a program with a complete manual for procedures. Every Monday night several faithful members of the church would conduct community outreach "according to the book."

After nearly two decades, however, the community changed. Though members detected resentment from residents they visited unannounced, the outreach program remained the same. The members had been doing it this way for years and change was difficult. "The rut" was dug for a good reason initially; but now the church was figuratively "spinning its wheels" and going nowhere.

3. Comfort

People need stability. A life with no routine or landmarks can be a life of stress and pain. It is understandable that many of our church members resist change. Too much change can lead to unwanted stress.

On the other hand, a life of the status quo can be equally harmful. Peter reminds us that we are "aliens and strangers in the world" (1 Pet. 2:11). We are to be like Abraham who, "by faith . . . made his home in the promised land like a stranger in a foreign country" (Heb. 11:9). We are not to become too comfortable in this world but, like Abraham, be willing to leave those comforts that mean the most to us (Gen. 12:1).

We often dig ruts in our Christian pilgrimage because we get too comfortable. And even a comfort as seemingly noble as an outreach program, a type of worship service, or a particular Sunday School class can become an idol if it keeps us out of the freshness of God's plan for our lives.

4. Misunderstood Purpose

Though comfort and routine partially explained Second Faith's entrenchment in a particular type of outreach program, the reason behind their failure to change was greater than those two explanations. A survey done of the active members in the church revealed this problem. When asked what they saw as their primary purpose for being a member of Second Faith, many of the members gave answers like: "To be involved in the outreach program" or "To be a teacher in the Sunday School."

The use of these words reveal a misunderstood purpose. The people were not called to be in a particular type of outreach or Sunday School program as much as they were called to reach others for Christ and to teach Christians the Bible. The difference in my words from theirs is more than semantics. The people of Second Faith saw their calling tied to a particular program rather than a ministry of outreach or teaching. God will change methods but He will never change His mission. It is a misunderstood purpose when a calling is tied to a methodology.

5. Lack of an Alternative

A church where I was pastor was stuck in a rut early in my ministry. We were involved in an outreach program that was simply ineffective. I made the decision to abandon the program. I received almost no criticism for that move because the ineffectiveness of the program was apparent to most of our members. The problem I created, however, was not being prepared to offer an alternative outreach ministry. We lost much of our outward focus because we went from an ineffective outreach to no outreach. At least in the ineffective program, our people were outwardly focused. My actions proved premature and costly.

The beauty of the vision cycle is that alternative approaches are discovered prior to the dissolution of old organizations and structures. A structure is created after ministry and growth is evident. In traditional churches we often create a new program (structure) with the high hopes that it will work. In the vision cycle the new ministry is already at work before a structure is implemented.

Three Prominent Examples

As I have visited other churches across our nation, I have discovered perhaps as many as twenty-five common "ruts" in which churches are unable to move. There are three prominent examples, however, which are common in a majority of traditional churches.

1. Worship Services

In the introduction to this book you met pastor Steve Cox. Steve created a lot of problems at First Community Church when he introduced some changes to the worship service. He thought the changes were mild. Many members of the church thought they were radical. Why do changes in worship service engender so much controversy? Three major perceptions explain the tension.

First, worship service equals church. For many members in our traditional churches, the worship service is the church. How many times do we hear someone say "I am going to Sunday School and church," when the latter refers to the Sunday morning worship service? Since the worship service is the time most members are assembled at once, it becomes the equivalent of the church.

This unfortunate terminology and misperception can create a great resistance to change. When the order of service is changed, when a contemporary hymn is introduced, when a new service is added, when a new pulpit is ordered, you have not just changed a worship service— you have changed the church. Old methodologies are grasped tenaciously if it is perceived that the church has been violated.

One statement cannot be repeated too often to the people of your church: The people are the church. They do not come to church on Sunday. They are the church seven days a week.

Second, worship services represent a rich heritage. When this statement explains resistance to changes in the worship service, the motive is a bit more understandable. Throughout the Old Testament, God reminded the people of Israel of the heritage He had given them (Josh. 1:6-9). Feasts and monuments were often established as a reminder of the goodness and faithfulness of God.

Many Christians are reminded of God's faithfulness in classic hymns and precise orders of worship. The traditionalists may genuinely hear the voice of God in hymns of old. Such sentiment should not be taken lightly.

59

Third, worship services have an uncertain purpose. Much of the tension in styles of worship services can be traced to conflicting opinions about the purpose of the worship services. Many people in traditional churches demonstrate through their words and actions that the worship services should be designed around the needs of the members. Thus when a traditionalist objects to a change in the worship service, what he or she is really saying is that you are not meeting his or her needs.

Others in the church may believe that the worship services should be designed as a means of outreach. At some churches, for example, many of the young families in the church express the need for more contemporary music as a means for reaching young Christian families moving into our community. "I cannot invite my friends," they contend, "unless we have something to offer them."

Yet some church members feel that worship services should have a strong evangelistic emphasis. A worship service with elements designed to reach non-Christians may be significantly different from one planned around the needs of members.

A church that finds itself in a "rut" with worship services planned for its members may encounter little open conflict. But the outreach potential of the service is lost in the comfort of this routine. One necessary warning: Any changes in this area should be taken with God's wisdom and at an elephant-eating pace. Remember Pastor Steve Cox in the introduction. For many of your church members, if you change the worship service, you will be tampering with *the* church.

2. Sunday School

The Sunday School can be a common organizational rut. If it is done well, the Sunday School program can be a dynamic organization for growth and ministry. I am not among those who predict the replacement of Sunday School with off-campus small groups. The program can be, however, stale and inefficient if it is not constantly worked and given fresh and new input.

Almost every traditional church has one or more Sunday School classes that would rather die than divide. And usually the former does take place. A class without a vision to grow and bring in new people will soon become lifeless and inwardly focused. C. Peter Wagner coined the word *koinonitis* to refer to groups that always look inward.[1] These groups have a tight fellowship among themselves, but entry into the group is next to impossible.

One pastor shared with me a story about one of the Sunday School classes in his church. Every member of the class had a high-back, cushioned chair (purchased with funds in the class treasury) with their name on it! And there were no other chairs in the classroom! The class might as well have placed a sign on the door that said "Outsiders Not Welcome."

The problem with *koinonitis* is that most groups will not admit that the "disease" exists in their fellowship. After all, they are a friendly people. Unfortunately their friendliness is limited to their group.

Without a continuous flow of new classes and new teachers, the Sunday School organization will become mired in a rut. And sadly ministry and growth will cease.

3. The Building

I recently read a news story about a small group of church members who refused to leave their church building after it had been condemned by the city. The few remaining members could not afford to make the many necessary repairs, and their numbers had grown smaller every year. For this group the building was the church. They had lost sight of the biblical truth that they were the church.

It is amazing how Christians can become so attached to a church's physical facilities and its furniture and fixtures. In my first small church in rural Indiana, I was about to preach my first sermon as the church's new pastor. Just before I spoke dear old Mrs. Smith exclaimed: "Turn on Jesus!" Thinking that the sweet lady was just being a bit emotional, I attempted again to begin my message. Once again she shouted: "Turn on Jesus!" Finally, a deacon came to my aid with a clarification of the mandate. Behind the pulpit was an old painting of Jesus with a single bulb to illuminate the picture. It was Mrs. Smith's belief that no preaching should take place until the cord was plugged in to provide electricity to illuminate the painting. Before every message thereafter, I "turned on Jesus."

Neither the building nor any of its components are the church, but many faithful church members will argue otherwise. When our focus becomes the physical facilities, we have become mired in yet another structural and organizational rut.

Three Cardinal Principles

We will return to the vision cycle once more. Clearly the way "out of the rut" is to move from a focus on the organization and structure to an outward focus. The mistake made by many leaders of traditional churches is to attack the organization and structure rather than refocus the church. The root of the problem is not the constitution and by-laws, the building, or the untouchable Sunday School class. The problem is a focus which is inward instead of outward. As you lead your church to become more outwardly focused, the following three principles should be of value:

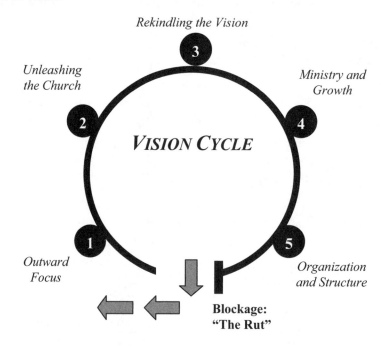

**GETTING "OUT OF THE RUT"
TO AN OUTWARD FOCUS**

1. Do Not Attack Friends of the Family

Short-term tenure in a church is often the result of violating this first principle. The "friend of the family" may be the tenaciously stubborn

62

couples' Sunday School class. Or it may be the monthly business meeting that attracts at least 5 percent of the church members. Remember the way out of the rut is not the attack of the rut itself. It is a new outward focus that helps people look beyond themselves.

2. It is Often Better to Add Than Subtract or Divide

In my former pastorates, we stopped dividing Sunday School classes. Instead we would seek a gifted teacher and a few "missionaries" from other classes. They would form the core for a new class. We would not divide another class; instead we would add a new class. It is fascinating to witness the excitement a new group brings to the entire organization. These new classes become the fastest-growing groups in the church. Outsiders are attracted to their newness and enthusiasm. And we have not depleted our emotional resources fighting the battles that are commensurate with making major changes in an existing group. Indeed it is often easier to add than to divide or subtract.

We encourage new groups to form where existing structures, committees, and organizations are "stuck in a rut." We do not disband the old groups. (That usually takes care of itself.) We simply start new groups to get the job done.

3. The Best Way to Handle an Obstacle Is to Go Around It

"Choose your battles," a wise pastor told me when I answered God's call to vocational ministry. "You will have the support of the church only if you carefully select the battles worth fighting. You cannot fight them all," another ministry veteran told me.

The traditional church offers both opportunities and obstacles. The obstacles are often the result of doing things the same way for years. And the obstacles may take the form of an organization, a methodology, a routine, or a person.

When you are confronted with an obstacle, three options are available. First you can let the obstacle stop you and stay where you are. Nothing will change. There will be times when such a retreat is wise. The timing to move forward may not be God's timing.

A second option is to fight the obstacle, to confront it head-on. Indeed such a confrontation or battle may be in order. I remember a church where a staff member was doing everything he could to undermine the pastor's work. After approaching the problem from

63

several different angles, the pastor finally had to give the staff member an ultimatum: get on the team or leave. Ultimately the staff member was dismissed. The process was painful but necessary. The pastor had a reputation of choosing his battles carefully. The church supported him in this tough decision.

Most obstacles can be handled, however, by going around them. In the first option nothing changes. In the second option the change comes at a great cost. In this third option change can be implemented without a major confrontation.

One Georgia church was in a new-growth area. Once a small town, the community in which the church was located had be-come a growing bedroom community for Atlanta commuters. The church seemed poised for growth except for an outreach leader who refused to change methodologies to reach these baby-boomer commuters. The pastor and staff simply began an additional outreach ministry and allowed the outreach leader to keep doing things his way. The church grew and, in time, the reluctant leader joined the team in the new and successful approach.

One Final Word about Ruts: Remember the Elephant

The ruts of the traditional church can come in all depths and with multiple levels of resistance. Some can be easily overcome; others take time to overcome. Remember the elephant. In a traditional church the best long-term successes often come when the problem is tackled methodically and with patience. You may be dealing with something that is of great emotional value to some church members.

Yet, at the same time, do not let the obstacles and ruts hinder your leadership from moving the church forward. The process may be slow, but it can be done. The greatest victories will come when you see a new outward focus and enthusiasm among your people.

NOTES

1. C. Peter Wagner, *Your Church Can Be Healthy* (Nashville: Abingdon, 1979), 87.

CHAPTER 4

VISION PRINCIPLES AND METHODS FOR YOUR CHURCH

"The main thing
is to make the main thing
the main thing."
-- unknown

Before we proceed further in the discussion of leading an established church to growth, we will pause to look at some critical principles for the vision of your church. This chapter will offer in summary both non-negotiable principles and methodological principles. These guidelines and prayer should be kept in mind as you lead your church to growth.

Ten Non-negotiable Principles

If you are like many church leaders, you have read several books or articles dealing with church growth. Many of these publications share exciting, new methodologies and principles which seem to engender growth. Some critics, however, have rightly pointed out that some of the methodologies are discussed with little biblical or theological foundation. The church growth writers are not necessarily unbiblical. They are simply assuming without articulating biblical truths.

Before we discuss any more methodological principles, I think we need to be absolutely clear about some biblical principles for growth that are non-negotiable. We may change our methods, but these truths are eternal and unchanging.

1. The Glory of God Is Our Motivation

The apostle Paul told the Corinthian church: "Whether you eat or drink, or whatever you do, do all to the glory of God" (1 Cor. 10:31). We who are church leaders must continually ask ourselves: "What is my motivation in leading my church?" In our eagerness to grow churches we can look at the growth and its numerical results as our goal. The numbers can take on an importance that is not from God. We are first children of God and then leaders of the church. In both roles nothing is more important than bringing glory to our Lord.

2. God Is in Total Control

One of the greatest assurances I have as a Christian and church leader is that God is sovereign, which means that He is in absolute control (Eph. 1:11). Many times in my own ministry I have seen the spontaneity of the Holy Spirit's work, which defies any plan or methodology. Such sovereign displays by God remind me that He is in control and that my church is really His church.

God's sovereign decree does not violate humankind's free will, nor does it make it unnecessary to seek methods of church growth. While Paul proclaimed with fervor the sovereignty of God, he also proclaimed with equal conviction the necessity of human intervention and preaching for church growth (Acts 16:13; Rom. 10:14-15; 1 Cor. 9:16). When we use methods in obedience to spread the gospel of Jesus Christ, we do not contradict the truth of God's sovereignty. One of the great joys of our faith is that God desires that we might be intermediaries in sharing the good news of His Son.

3. Christ Is the Only Way

As I write this chapter, I am in the middle of a media controversy. In an unusual twist of events, my denomination's belief that Christ is the only way of salvation has suddenly become newsworthy. Various local and national media have interviewed me about "Southern Baptist beliefs." What I have attempted to tell these interviewers is that the exclusiveness of salvation through Christ is not first a Southern Baptist belief. It is a biblical truth that came from the words of Jesus Himself (John 14:6). The truth of the cross is offensive to the world.

In our enthusiasm to lead churches to growth, we must never compromise this truth. The fact that Christ is the *only* way and that hell is a real consequence for those who reject Him is not a "user-friendly" concept. But it is truth, and it must be communicated.

4. Christ Builds the Church

The issue of jealousy between leaders of different churches is a real one. I am sure that every person who reads these pages can think of a church which is growing more rapidly than their own. More times than many of us would like to admit, our carnal nature evokes feelings of jealousy and inadequacy when we hear of such churches.

A kingdom mind-set, however, sees things differently. First, all Christian churches are Christ's churches. Second, Jesus is the builder of churches, not ourselves. In His historic discussion with Peter, Jesus said, "I will build *my* church" (Matt. 16:18, author's emphasis). We are in the kingdom business, and we all work for the same Master. There is no room for jealousy and competitive spirits.

5. The Bible Is Our Authority

I appreciate your reading this book. It has been my prayer while writing it that God would use the book to reach people for Christ and to encourage church leaders. Indeed you have access to many outstanding books on the church and leadership.

All such church growth resources and tools may be beneficial to you and your church. The tools of church growth are not inherently evil, as some critics imply. But, these tools and resources must always be within the bounds of Scripture and subject to biblical authority. The Bible is our authority, and it is our ultimate church growth book.

6. Church Growth Is Spiritual Warfare

Satan will do everything he can to prevent you from leading your church to growth. Every soul saved by Christ is a soul that will not be with Satan in hell. Paul knew that warfare for the evangelistic, church-growing Christian was inevitable: "For our struggle is not against flesh and blood, but against the rulers, against the authorities, against the powers of this dark world and against the spiritual forces of evil in the heavenly realms" (Eph. 6:12).

Satan and his demons have many weapons which they use to inhibit the growth of the church. They can deceive both believers and unbelievers. Unbelievers can be deceived and blinded from receiving the gift of salvation through Jesus Christ: "The god of this age has blinded the minds of the unbelievers, so that they cannot see the light of the gospel of the glory of Christ, who is the image of God" (2 Cor. 4:4). A believer can also be distracted from Great Commission obedience and single-minded devotion to Christ (11:3). The apostle Paul, concerned that the church of the Thessalonians might have lost zeal for spreading the gospel, wrote to warn the people about demonic discouragement: "For this reason, when I could stand it no longer, I sent to find out about your faith. I was afraid that in some way the tempter might have tempted you and our efforts might have been useless" (1 Thess. 3:5).

In Paul's words about spiritual warfare in Ephesians 6, he instructs us about our weapons to combat the forces of the evil one. He calls these weapons "the full armor of God" (v. 13). The full armor first includes a godly and obedient lifestyle ("righteousness . . . readiness . . . faith," vv. 14-16). Second, it means a knowledge of, commitment to, and obedience to the Word of God ("the sword of the Spirit, which is the Word of God," v. 17). Finally, the full armor leads us to prayer (v. 18). We look at that vital principle next.

7. Prayer Is a Key Church Growth Principle

Prayer should be a priority in the church because God's Word mandates it. Even if we could find no positive correlation between prayer and church growth, the mandate of prayer would require our obedience. It is fascinating, however, to learn how God is working through prayer to lead churches to unprecedented levels of growth. In one study of churches which had reversed their negative growth rate, the key factor for the reversal was determined to be an increased emphasis on prayer. The prayers of the early church unleashed the power of God to add thousands to the church. It happened then, and it is happening in many churches today. We believe so much in the power and priority of prayer that we are devoting the next chapter to this critical issue. We believe so much in the power and priority of prayer that we are devoting the next chapter to this critical issue.

8. The Church Is Still Important

In my first pastorate, I visited a lady who had not attended our church in over a decade. Though a longtime member, she did not see the need for attending her church. She was well prepared for my visit. "Pastor," she said condescendingly, "I have discovered that God and I have a much better relationship when I do not attend church. Those hypocrites mess up my spiritual growth." I wish I had had the intestinal fortitude to say that she would have fit in nicely with the rest of us hypocrites.

One of the unavoidable truths of the New Testament is that the local church is important in God's plan. The writer of Hebrews made clear God's intention for believers to gather and work together: "Let us not give up meeting together, as some are in the habit of doing, but let us encourage one another—and all the more as you see the Day approaching" (Heb. 10:25). Even more than single passages, large blocks of Scripture (1 Cor. 12-14) point to the importance of a gathered, united, and serving church. The majority of the books of the New Testament are particularly concerned with local church issues.

Despite the imperfections of those who comprise the local church, it is still God's primary vehicle for calling the world to Himself. Indeed the church is the body of Christ (12:27).

9. Evangelism Is Still the Priority

Many times I will lead a conference and begin a discussion on ministries in the church. I may discuss social ministries or discipleship ministries in general, or I may refer to some particular ministry. Typically I receive a surprised look when I share the most effective means to lead a church in discipleship and social ministries: Have a priority for evangelism.

How can a church with a priority for evangelism be a church with dynamic social and discipleship ministries? First, let us examine the biblical evidence. Our Lord Jesus Christ, who taught us the perfect plan for discipling and providing for needs, did so within a context that placed the eternal state of a person as more important than the temporal state: "If your right eye causes you to sin, gouge it out and throw it away. It is better for you to lose one part of your body than for your whole body to be thrown into hell" (Matt. 5:29). Again, the words of Jesus seem to favor an evangelistic priority: "Do not be afraid of those who kill the body but cannot kill the soul. Rather, be afraid of the One who can destroy both soul and body in hell" (10:28).

The historical and contemporary evidence seems to support this thesis: *A greater evangelistic emphasis and higher evangelistic priority*

69

will enhance all ministries of the church. (Remember the outward focus point on the vision cycle is the first movement away from organizational and structural stagnation.) A landmark study of evangelists and revivalists in the nineteenth century found that though the well-known evangelists held to a priority of winning people to Christ, they were also instrumental in initiating massive social reforms.[1]

Yet another major study in the 1960s came to that same conclusion. The modern evangelical movement, while holding a priority of evangelism, was also maintaining a strong social conscience.[2] Even as we head into the twenty-first century, the same evidence is repeated: churches that emphasize evangelism tend to have a greater awareness of social and discipleship needs.[3]

Yet on the other hand, we can look at the records of mainline denominations that have lost their evangelistic zeal and priority. Their numerical decline has been the subject of countless studies. Within those same studies, however, there has been a noted decline in resources for other ministries which has impacted negatively those areas deemed to be of highest importance. A low priority for evangelism is detrimental to the entire ministry of the church.

One entire Christian movement collapsed as it rearranged its priorities away from evangelism. The Student Volunteer Movement was founded early in the twentieth century upon the slogan: "The evangelization of the world in this generation." Many Christian leaders enthusiastically endorsed the movement as the single most potent force for missions in America in the early part of the century. Yet, in the 1940s the organization ceased to exist. Its original priority of evangelism had shifted to new emphases such as race relations, international relationships, and economic justice. Not only did the collapse of the movement cause a major evangelistic thrust to end, it also thwarted an emphasis on many other worthy ministries and causes.

10. The Laity Must Do the Ministry

I once ran into a friend who had pastored his church for seventeen years. He had followed many of the principles cited in this book. But, for the past four years, his church had plateaued after many years of steady growth. He and I both realized the major problem immediately after we looked at the vision cycle. For all practical purposes he had not led the church and the people to be unleashed for ministry. The church had grown well for years despite skipping this step. But now the church did not have enough leaders in ministry to care for all the people and to involve new people. Neither assimilation nor discipleship was taking place.

The beauty of the church in Acts was the picture of every believer being involved in ministry. A person not involved in ministry would not have been considered a part of the church. A Christian, by his or her very nature, would be doing ministry. How that scenario has changed in most American churches! Before we conclude this chapter you will read of some possible tools for unleashing the laity. The most important thing your church leaders can do is to begin now equipping others for ministry. That is your biblical mandate (Eph. 4:11-12). You may have to begin small, working with one or two others. Then those two will be equipped to equip others. The process will be slow, especially in an established church. By eating small bites of the elephant slowly, progress will be made toward devouring the entire creature!

Methodological Principles for Growth

In the previous section of this chapter we saw some non-negotiable principles for growth. Now we will examine some methodologies that may prove to be beneficial in leading your church to growth.

The Church Growth Movement has been instrumental in introducing new methods that can help churches grow and reach people for Christ. These methodological principles truly have been used of God for His kingdom. Methods, however, are only for a season. Remember the exciting method of busing? Thousands of people, primarily children, were introduced to the Savior by this method in the sixties and early seventies. Today, however, very few churches have a large busing ministry.

Many critics of church growth today are accusing the movement of being overzealous in promoting methods without a sound theology. I can understand the concern of the critics. We must place methods in their place: tools that we are using for a season under the watch of a sovereign God.

71

If you sense that the Lord is leading you in a certain direction, the application of methods must be timed with wisdom from God. For traditional or established churches, the introduction of new tools may need to be taken in "bite-sized" steps.

On the other hand, as you lead your church on the vision cycle, perhaps many of the "sacred cows" of the church can be seen as outdated and nonessential methodology. Many churches today have a worship service near the 11:00 A.M. hour on Sundays. The timing of this service was implemented decades ago as a new methodology to meet the needs of an agricultural nation, particularly those farmers with dairy cattle that needed early-morning milkings!

So, as you read or review some of the latest church growth methodologies, think about them with discernment from God. Are they right for your church? Are your people ready for their application? Are there better methodologies to meet your purpose? Will the benefits of the new methods exceed the potential problems? Perhaps the greatest danger of a well-meaning church leader hearing about new methods would be his or her uncritical application of them to the church. Ask God for wisdom. He promises that He will deliver (Jas. 1:5).

Evangelism Methods

"How do we do evangelism in our society today?" Pastor Nail asked. "The methods we used in the past to win people to Christ are just not as effective today. Where do we go from here?"

Pastor Nail's questions have been asked thousands of times by church leaders across our nation. "Cold-call" visitation and evangelistic confrontations are becoming more and more difficult to accomplish. Several changes in our society explain the new paradigm in evangelistic methods.

First, our society is becoming more pagan. The Judeo-Christian value system is not accepted by the vast numbers as was evident in earlier years. Whereas many unsaved people in the 1950s and 1960s would at least be receptive to the gospel message, today the message of the cross is just one of multiple options. In our present age, much "pre-evangelism" must often take place just to win a hearing.

Second, we live in an unbelievably fast-paced society. Time has become Americans' most valuable commodity.[4] Innovators in marketing have understood this need and have given us the Internet, computers, microwaves, cellular phones, fax machines, automated teller machines, fast foods, home deliveries, and convenience stores.

Part of the explanation behind the loss of time is the number of women in the work force. More than half of all women now work outside the home.[5] With both husband and wife employed, time becomes more and more scarce. Evangelism methods of earlier years, such as cold-call confrontations, are now viewed by many as a rude invasion of privacy and a theft of time.

Third, Christianity to many people today simply seems irrelevant. The language, methodology, music, organizations, buildings, and sermons often do not reflect the world in which most people live. A walk into a church (if we could really get them into the front door) would be a trip into a nostalgic past at best and boring irrelevance at worst.

How, then, do we reach this fast-paced, confused society for Christ? First, we must understand that society in general is less receptive to the gospel. James Engel developed a linear scale to help us understand better the unbeliever's resistance or receptivity to the message of salvation.[6]

-8 Awareness of a supreme being, but no effective knowledge of the gospel
-7 Initial awareness of the gospel
-6 Awareness of the fundamentals of the gospel
-5 Grasp of the implications of the gospel
-4 Positive attitude toward the gospel
-3 Personal problem recognition
-2 Decision to act
-1 Repentance and faith in Christ

✝ The person is regenerated and becomes a new creature.

+1 Post-decision evaluation
+2 Incorporation into the body
+3 A lifetime of conceptual and behavioral growth in Christ

Most churches that have an evangelistic thrust approach lost persons as if they are "-4" or "-3" on the Engel scale. Such an assumption would have been fair three decades ago. Today a larger number of people are "-8" or "-7" on the scale. If we are to be effective evangelists, we must recognize that most people are a lot further from the cross than they were a few decades earlier. How can we reach these people for Christ in our traditional churches? What are some first steps in moving our people toward an outward focus for evangelistic results on the vision cycle? The key, it seems, will be methods which enhance the development of relationships between believers and unbelievers.

Small Groups. The small group may be the most effective evangelistic tool of the twenty-first century. A small group can be an evangelistically focused Sunday School class (unfortunately most Sunday School classes do not fit this description) or an off-campus group. Our relationship-hungry society is often willing to go into homes and other "neutral" sites for Bible studies and topical studies.

Flexible Worship Services. The traditional church may be able to move slowly into an additional worship service. This new service could be designed specifically to reach lost people (seeker-driven services) or to be sensitive to the needs of lost people (seeker-sensitive services). Services that are flexible in day, time, and format can be a tremendous evangelistic tool. The caution, of course, is for a traditional church to proceed deliberately in planning such services.

Ministry-based Evangelism. The need for the Savior is the greatest need for humanity. Yet, much of the time, other more temporal needs must be met to gain a hearing. Many churches have successfully implemented ministries which have an evangelistic emphasis. Speaking in terms of the Engel scale, those churches have helped individuals more from, for example, a "-7" (initial awareness of the gospel) to a "-4" (positive attitude toward the gospel). Such individuals may soon be receptive to a verbal presentation of the gospel.[7]

Evangelism Training. While cold-call evangelism may not always be the most effective means of reaching people for Christ, it will continue to have its place. All Christians will be placed in situations where they should be ready to share Christ verbally. A brief encounter with the person on the airplane is but one common example. And even

74

in those times where a relationship has developed between a believer and an unbeliever, the Christian must eventually present the gospel clearly.

For these reasons, churches should continue to provide evangelism training. About 10 percent of the active adult membership may be willing to participate in in-depth evangelistic training programs. The leadership of the church should provide less-intensive methods of training for the rest of the body.

A traditional church with a healthy balance of evangelistic emphases will thus encourage means by which the members can develop relationships with unbelievers, while equipping the people with specific evangelistic training. And some traditional churches may be ready to introduce a new worship service that has a sensitivity to unbelievers.

Laity Involvement Methods

Besides being biblically obedient, the involvement of the laity in ministry has many immediate benefits to the church:

- ✔ Pastors and other staff members are freed to do other ministries, especially prayer and study of the Word (Acts 6:4);
- ✔ The number of ministries increases proportionally to additional lay involvement;
- ✔ Involvement of the laity in ministry is a great assimilation method. Those who are involved rarely leave the church or become inactive;
- ✔ Involved people are happy people. Malcontents rarely come from the ranks of those involved in ministry;
- ✔ People who do ministry are typically generous financial supporters of the church. They see the benefits of their tithes and offerings.

Only insecure leaders would thwart attempts of the people of the church to become involved in dynamic ministries. Most of you reading the benefits just listed are undoubtedly desiring them for your churches. But how can such unleashing of the church take place? Are any methods particularly effective today? Here are some methods that are effective in involving our church members in dynamic and exciting ministries.

Established Programs. Despite the less-than-enthusiastic reviews given to established programs, such programs may still be one of the most effective means to get the people off the pews and into the front lines of ministry. What is meant by "established programs"? It refers to ministries or equipping methods that are implemented by a person or an agency other than those who are involved in the program. For example, your denomination may have a great video series on prayer ministry that can be shown and discussed in your church. Several of your members may hear God speak through the videotapes and ensuing discussion and, as a result, become involved in a dynamic prayer ministry in your church.

Never underestimate the power of established programs to involve people in ministry. While many of the books on the market today speak of new and innovative approaches to ministry, I still see the need to thank God for programs that change lives who in turn change more lives.

Lay-started Ministries. Over the past several years, many church leaders have realized that programs alone may not open all the doors God has planned for the people of the church. God often speaks directly to His people to start ministries which are not part of the church's programs.

Several years ago some laypersons in a church I served in Birmingham, Alabama became concerned about hunger among the poorer families in our area. Because Green Valley is a relatively affluent suburb of Birmingham, we rarely saw economically deprived families visit our church. The concerned laypeople in the church decided that we could minister to these people even if they never set foot in one of our services.

From this burden a small ministry was begun to provide food to a few hurting families. Today the Food Bank ministry of Green Valley Baptist is one of the largest such ministries in metropolitan Birmingham. Thousands of families have been fed and years later, a large clothing ministry was started to augment the food ministry. Of all the ministries in our church, only the Sunday School involves more people.

What are some key principles involved in seeing exciting lay-started ministries implemented? First, the people of the church must know that they are free to respond to God's call. Many churches are mired down in thick layers of rules and bureaucracies. Starting something new requires so much bureaucratic action that the member can quickly become discouraged. The leader should work patiently within the system, encouraging the member until such time as the structures can be changed.

Second, the pastor, staff, or some small leadership team still needs to be a permission-granting authority. While most new ministries should be approved, a safeguard for unacceptable and far-out proposals needs to be in place. Caution is warranted here. Leaders need to be very careful that they do not take on the role of the Holy Spirit. A member's sense of call from God needs to be taken seriously. My staff and I sometimes erred on the side of permission-granting rather than permission-withholding.

Third, the leaders should equip the people for ministry. Books, seminars, videotapes, classes, and referrals to others with similar ministries are some good starting points.

Finally, the leader of the new ministry should remain accountable to another leader in the church, possibly the pastor or another staff member. The ministry then should be evaluated on a regular basis.

Determining Community Needs. The laity may further become involved in ministry when they discover needs in the community. It is amazing to see Christians respond when they become aware of a need!

How does need awareness happen in a church? The simplest but most often neglected principle is the communication of needs by the pastor or other leaders to the people. We church leaders so often try to carry the burden of ministry alone while many people are waiting to be asked to help.

Another excellent method is the community survey described in chapter 2. I encourage you to return to that chapter and read again the methodology of the survey. The tool can excite your people about doing ministry!

Physical Facilities as Tools

First Evangelical Church was growing at a remarkable pace. After overflow crowds cramped the tiny one-hundred-seat worship center in two of their three morning worships, the church voted to build. Excitement mounted during the early planning stages, the stewardship campaign, and the actual construction of the four-hundred-seat facility. Finally the project was completed and an overflow crowd came to the dedication service. But one year later attendance settled to 225 and showed no signs of increasing.

How could a church with such dynamic growth hit a plateau so quickly? The building program scenario and its aftermath are, unfortunately, common occurrences. The church focuses most of its spiritual, financial, and emotional resources upon the project. And when the project is complete, the emotional letdown often follows. The church has misplaced its focus. "The building" has become synonymous with "the church." The people no longer see themselves as the body of Christ. They go *to* church rather than realize that *they are* the church.

I am hesitant to mention the building and other physical facilities as a church growth tool since so many churches place undue importance upon them. Quite frankly, I have seen churches in pathetic facilities reach many for Christ. And I have seen churches with their own Taj Mahals have absolutely no interest in reaching people for the kingdom. Having said that, I will now mention two basic growth concerns regarding physical facilities: space and appearance.

Space. An often-cited principle of church growth is that when 80 percent of any facility is in use, it is time to make provisions for more room. The rule-of-thumb applies typically to five areas: parking, sanctuary, land, nursery (preschool), and education space. When large malls are built, owners make certain their facilities are never completely filled, except perhaps during two or three holiday periods. The owners want passersby to know that additional parking is always available and convenient. Such a mentality is common among churchgoers today. A packed sanctuary or parking lot sends the message that there is no more room.

Where are space constraints most critical? Parking must be included near the top. Some churches are attempting innovative parking approaches such as shuttle parking or valet parking.

For those churches desiring to reach young families, adequate preschool space is a must. Today's discerning parents hesitate to leave their children in a room with wall-to-wall preschoolers. Following the need for adequate preschool space is education space for older children, youth, and, finally, adults.

You may have noticed that the list of space priorities did not include the sanctuary. Because of the relative ease of having multiple worship services, new sanctuary space should not be considered a high priority until the church has utilized the space with at least two or three worship services. Such a perspective is difficult for both church leaders and members to accept quickly. Many members prefer one service where everyone is together. And many leaders would rather lead their church in a building program for such a visible edifice as a sanctuary. Church members have a tendency to support the building of a sanctuary with their financial resources more so than other projects. But if reaching people for Christ and being a good steward of God's money are your priorities, other needs will come first.

Appearance. When I served as pastor, every six months I asked a person who had never seen our church to walk inside and outside our facilities. If possible, this person would not be active in a church so that he or she could give us a perspective that a non-believer may have. I asked the person to take notes, give first impressions and be critical where applicable. To some degree, we needed to be concerned that our churches exude quality. An unsaved person should be able to walk into our churches and see that Christians care about their facilities. An unkempt church may convey a lackadaisical attitude about other matters to the unchurched.

Planning and Goal Setting as Tools

A study of growing churches revealed a surprisingly strong correlation between planning and goal setting and the growth of the church.[8] Planning is a common-sense good use of the resources God has given us. It increases efficiency in the church as God's resources of time, energy, and money are best used for good stewardship.

Planning also helps the entire church team understand the vision and the process necessary to accomplish the vision. Similarly, planning engenders accountability as progress is measured according to the plan.

The key elements of an effective plan are vision, goals (by-products of the vision), strategies, communication, and evaluation. It is the element of goal-setting that motivates the church to put a plan into action. In many ways, a goal is a measure of faith. Goal-setting is a way to refocus and to dream again.

Goal setting, if it is both challenging and realistic, can produce motivation and excitement. Leaders must realize that most church members are hungering to be a part of a church that makes a difference. If those members can see real evidence that the church and its leadership are committed to new and challenging directions, enthusiasm will be natural and spontaneous.

Seeing the Methods on the Vision Cycle

Two cautions about using methods should be mentioned at this point. First, your church's readiness for a new method must be a matter of prayer and discernment. Numerous times thus far in the book we have cited the dangers of moving too rapidly in an established church. Prayerful patience is important.

Second, we must know why we are utilizing methods. Is the method designed to give our church an outward focus? Is the method a tool for unleashing the laity? Is it a new organization or structure designed to accommodate new growth and ministries? Or, have we chosen methods that turn the church inward rather than outward?

One of the major mistakes of church leaders today in methodological application is using a certain method for the wrong reason. As an example, let us return to the vision cycle (see the next page) and look at the methods mentioned in this chapter.

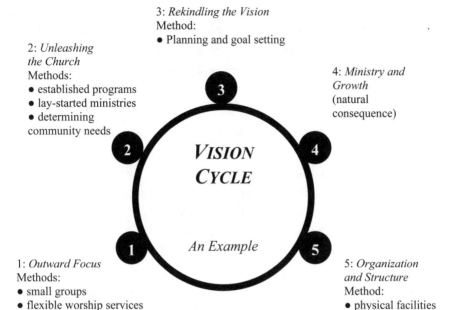

3: *Rekindling the Vision*
Method:
- Planning and goal setting

2: *Unleashing the Church*
Methods:
- established programs
- lay-started ministries
- determining community needs

4: *Ministry and Growth*
(natural consequence)

VISION CYCLE

An Example

1: *Outward Focus*
Methods:
- small groups
- flexible worship services
- evangelism training

5: *Organization and Structure*
Method:
- physical facilities

METHODS ON THE VISION CYCLE

Now, let us look at Grace Evangelical Church. Pastor Jess Keller knows that the church is in a rut. Almost no growth has taken place in six years, and the people have no sense of outward focus. In an effort to revitalize the church, Pastor Keller comes up with the idea of building a new worship center. Though the space is adequate today, he believes a building program will bring new life into the church. The members will see the project as a way to draw others to the church. Pastor Keller is about to make a major mistake!

Look on the vision cycle. Physical facilities are tools for organization and structure. They accommodate ministry and growth that has already taken place. Such a method in no way engenders an outward focus. Architect and church consultant Ray Bowman knows that "conventional wisdom says that church buildings create growth."[9] But his forty years of experience working with churches tells otherwise: "Church buildings often kill church growth. In over forty years as a church architect and consultant, I have seen it happen time and again. An exciting, growing congregation builds to make room for

81

continued growth, only to see their growth stop as soon as they build."[10]

Bowman goes on to explain the phenomenon. I believe that you will see his words are in perfect agreement with the concept of a vision cycle:

> Now, I'm not against church buildings. After all, I am an architect. I have designed buildings for churches most of my life. *There is a right time and a right way to build.* But in far too many cases building programs have killed, or at least slowed, the growth of vital congregations. Why?

> A major reason is that the church's focus changes. Most church growth occurs because a church effectively ministers to people's needs. Its focus is on people. *But often, when a growing church builds, its focus shifts from people to building. That change of focus kills church growth.*[11]

Bowman further warns of three things church buildings can never do: stimulate growth, improve members' givings, and motivate people to minister. He is not condemning the use of buildings as a tool. His concern is the appropriate use of buildings as a tool. Clearly, it is not a method for an outward focus.

For every method we lead our churches to use, we must ask several questions. Is the timing right? Is the method the correct tool for the most urgent need of the church? And does the method complement the non-negotiable principles and theological framework in which our church ministers?

Tools and methods are not inherently evil. They can be used effectively in traditional churches with great results. But the use of such tools and the timing of their application must be from God. It is His wisdom we seek, not our own.

NOTES

1. See Timothy L. Smith, *Revivalism and Social Reform in Mid-Nineteenth-Century America* (New York: Abingdon, 1957).

2. See Sherwood Wirt, *The Social Conscience of the Evangelical* (New York: Harper and Row, 1968).

3. See C. Kirk Hadaway, *Church Growth Principles: Separating Fact From Fiction* (Nashville: Broadman, 1991).

4. George Barna, *The Frog in the Kettle* (Ventura, Calif: Regal, 1990), 39.

5. Ibid., 98.

6. The Engel scale can be found in many church growth books. The best explanation is found in C. Peter Wagner, *Strategies for Church Growth* (Ventura, Calif: Regal, 1987), 124.

7. *His Heart, Our Hands* is a good ministry evangelism toolkit available from the North American Mission Board, www.namb.net.

8. Hadaway, 114.

9. Ray Bowman with Eddy Hall, *When Not to Build* (Grand Rapids, Mich: Baker, 1992), 27.

10. Ibid.

11. Ibid., emphasis added.

83

CHAPTER 5

PRAYER—A NON-NEGOTIABLE

"Do not restrain prayer. . . . For only
through prayer can the prosperity of
a church be increased or even maintained."[1]
-- Charles Spurgeon

The conference was going well, I thought, until a local pastor expressed his aggravation with the "vision cycle" approach presented in this book. "It's just another business model brought into the church," he said. "Here's the philosophy. Just get your salesmen out of the office—to think more about the customer—and you might get more sales. You've forgotten that the church isn't a business!"

I suppose I could have overlooked the fact that this brother wrongly assumed that the church does not need to "get out of the office more." Most of us have become so cocooned in the church world that we do not even know many non-believers anymore.

I could have even ignored the possibility that this pastor was simply a church growth skeptic, always looking for some reason to criticize anything related to church growth. (I would have wondered why he had come to my conference, but I still could have heard his concern without becoming frustrated myself).

What bothered me about the pastor's remarks was that I had just spent an hour of the conference emphasizing the topic of this chapter: *the importance of prayer in moving a church through the vision cycle.* In fact, I had said specifically, "a church without the power of God is only a business, and prayer is a primary means by which we tap into His power"!

The goal of this chapter is to help your church implement an effective prayer strategy as you move toward growth. I hope that Charles Spurgeon's words at the beginning of this chapter will become your words as you read this section of this book.

The Importance of Prayer

Think for a minute about praying people in the Bible. Abraham prayed for a city (Gen. 18:20-33). Moses prayed for God's people (Exod. 32:11-13). Joshua prayed for guidance (Josh. 7:1-26). Hannah prayed for a child (1 Sam. 1:1-20). Solomon prayed for wisdom (1 Kgs. 3:1-15). The prophets of God prayed, too, for various reasons (e.g., 1 Kgs. 18:36-39; Jer. 20:7-18).

The early church—dependent on God as they were for all things— prayed fervently (Acts 1:14, 3:1, 4:31, 6:4, 10:9, 12:5, 13:3, 14:23, 16:25, 20:36, 28:8). The apostle Paul prayed for believers (e.g., Rom. 1:8, 1 Cor. 1:4), and he expected them to pray for him (Eph. 6:18-20, Col. 4:2-4). Jesus, of course, modeled a life of prayer for all of us (e.g., Matt. 26:36-46; Mark 1:35; Luke 4:42, 5:16, 6:12, 11:1; John 17).

Here's the point: prayer matters, and faithful believers are praying believers. And, as we have learned again and again in our research at the Billy Graham School, growing churches are praying churches.[2]

Yet, churches still struggle in developing effective prayer warriors and prayer ministries. I have the privilege of visiting in dozens of churches and working with hundreds of pastors each year. Seldom do I hear a pastor say, "My church just prays so much that it's hard to believe." More likely the question is, "What do I need to do to get my church to pray?"

If prayer matters so much, why do many churches not emphasize prayer?

Non-praying Churches Are Often Mis-Focused Churches.

You might suggest several reasons to explain why churches do not pray. Maybe they have not been trained to pray effectively. Perhaps the church does not have a praying leader. They might be so busy doing church that they do not take the time to pray.

All of these are possible causes for a non-praying church. Think, though, about these more foundational causes, especially as you consider the vision cycle.

Non-praying churches do not see a need to pray. Let's be honest. Most church leaders can do much of ministry in our own strength. Typically, we have enough training and enough ability to do the work of ministry without necessarily relying on the power of God. The result is a ministry without much eternal significance.

Churches are no different. They often have enough people and enough talent to do the work of the church, even if they are not praying as they should. How many churches do you know that meet Sunday after Sunday, year after year, and yet prayer is not an emphasis?

Because we *can* do church in our own power, we do. The work goes on ("organization and structure" on the vision cycle), but the power of God is not present.

Non-praying churches have sometimes been diverted from prayer. One of the churches I pastored recognized a need for more space. Because the cost of increased facilities was significant, we knew we needed to pray for wisdom. We prayed and sensed God's direction to renovate current space and complete an unfinished educational wing.

Looking back, I wonder if we prayed as much once the building process began. Plans were developed and approved. Contractors were hired. Volunteers were enlisted. The work was completed, but I'm not sure we bathed the finishing process in prayer. Instead, I think we diverted our attention from prayer to building.

How easily diversion happens, especially in the organization and structure phase of the vision cycle. We pray for God to give us workers, but do we pray as much for them when they are in place? We seek God's guidance in developing a church growth strategy, but do we pray as fervently after the strategy is adopted?

Non-praying churches have not been challenged with God-sized tasks. What has happened recently in your church that can be explained only by the power and presence of God? Has He challenged you to accept an assignment that your church cannot do without His power?

Randy Cheek is the pastor of the Ash Street Baptist Church near Atlanta, Georgia. Pastor Randy has challenged his church to pray for God to do something for which "no man can take any credit in any way." They have recognized the wisdom of Henry Blackaby in his popular work, *Experiencing God*:

Some people say, "God will never ask me to do something I can't do." I have come to the place in my life that, if the assignment I sense God is giving me is something that I know I can handle, I know it probably is not from God.[3]

It might be that moving your traditional, established church through the vision cycle is a God-sized task. Guiding a mis-focused church toward an outward focus is often quite a challenge. If that's the case in your church, do not fret. Accept the challenge, and pray to the God who can do all things!

Consider with me further why prayer matters so much for a church moving through the vision cycle.

Praying Churches Admit That They Are Powerless to Get Out of Ruts

Do you remember the story in chapter three about driving on south Alabama dirt roads? Several times, Dr. Rainer and his friends needed help to free their car after they had buried it in the mud of the rain-soaked roads.

That's the way it is with churches stuck in a rut—we need help from somebody else to get out of the rut. In this case, that "somebody else" is God (and who else would we want?).

You know the stories. First Church is stuck in a "we've never done it that way" philosophy, and no pastor has been successful in budging them. Second Church has had just enough success to brag—a new building and a lot of transfer growth—but getting them to reach out to unbelievers is like pulling the proverbial teeth. Third Church is just plain stuck. The organization is in place and the programs are functioning, but nothing "God-sized" is happening.

What do you think it will take to move these churches effectively through the vision cycle? Only God can do it, and prayer is the means through which He works.

Praying Churches Put Their Focus on God

One of my favorite verses in the creation story is Genesis 3:9— "Then the Lord called to the man, and said to him, 'Where are you?'" (NAS). This verse grabs me because *God came looking for Adam and*

Eve after they had sinned against Him. They had rejected His word, but He sought them anyway because He's always been an outward-focused God.

Prayer is about a relationship with this God, and praying churches focus on Him and on those He loves. A church simply can't focus on God through prayer and remain centered on themselves. My co-author, Thom Rainer, describes the process this way: "When a church emphasizes and organizes an intercessory prayer ministry, the focus of those praying moves from self to God to others."[4]

As I write this chapter, I have just completed an exciting weekend with an evangelical church in the western part of the United States. When I walked into their building, I immediately saw the flags of several nations hanging in their worship center. The flags represent countries to which the church has sent missionaries. It was not surprising that that same church had committed the weekend to fasting and praying for God's will to be done in their congregation. They had been in the practice of seeking God through prayer, and that God-centered focus had led them to be concerned about the world.

Praying Churches Learn to Persevere Patiently in Faith

Getting out of an organizational rut often takes more time than we hoped. It probably took a while to get into the rut in the first place, and climbing out also takes some time. Pastors Alan Nelson and Gene Appel remind us that "often, though not always, the longer a habit has been functioning, the longer it takes to change. . . . In general, the larger the change, the longer it will take to process the change effectively."[5] To state it another way, it's tough to eat an elephant in a hurry.

What does this fact have to do with prayer? Have you ever wondered why the Bible so often calls us to wait? (e.g., Isa. 40:31, Psa. 52:9, Acts 1:4). One reason must be that we are often impatient—we want God to respond to our needs in a microwave fashion. We church leaders want God to change our churches *right now.* Sometimes it even seems like we want the answers to our prayers before we ever pray the prayer!

Praying churches realize, though, that God's timing seldom matches our timing. He does not always respond as quickly as we would like—

but we can still trust Him to accomplish His plan. That lesson learned through persistent prayer can also encourage us to press on as we lead churches through the vision cycle. Eat the elephant *one bite at a time*, remembering that God always answers our prayers according to His timetable.

Principles for Developing a Prayer Ministry

Elsewhere I have written extensively about developing a prayer ministry in the local church.[6] My goal in this section is simply to describe three of the most basic prayer ministry principles described more completely in these other works.

1. The Pastor Must Set the Example

I served as a pastor for fourteen years before joining the faculty at Southern Seminary. During those years, I read as much as I could about prayer ministries (to be honest, in an attempt to find a quick-fix way to get my churches to pray more fervently). Imagine my conviction when I read words like these from the pastor of a growing church in Texas:

> For thirty years I preached more prayer than I prayed. But it wasn't until people started seeing praying in my life that my words made a difference. We are fighting on the wrong battlefield. The battle is to be won on our knees. Then we go out and do what God tells us to do. *There is no substitute for praying preachers.*[7]
> (emphasis added)

I wanted a ready-made program for prayer, but almost everything I read said that a praying church begins with a praying pastor. Combine that truth with research indicating that most pastors pray no more than an average of twenty-two minutes per day, and you see why the prayer life of most churches is anemic at best.[8]

My friend Rick Fisher is the pastor of Lexington Baptist Church in Lexington, South Carolina. This church is a praying church, led by a praying pastor. Pastor Rick will tell you that his own passion for prayer developed when he realized the "futility of attempting kingdom ministry with human strength and wisdom."[9] Ministry in his own power led to a lack of fulfillment and a lack of lasting fruit. Now, having learned that intimacy with God is critical, this pastor leads his church in corporate prayer gatherings, spiritual disciplines training, and an annual prayer conference. That continued focus on God, I suspect, helps keep this church out of the ruts.

2. A Prayer Coordinator Should Oversee the Ministry

Though the title differs from church-to-church (e.g., prayer director, minister of prayer, prayer leader), most congregations with effective prayer ministries have one member who oversees the ministry. Remember, *let the laity do the ministry.* The sample job description below might guide you as you seek this important leader.

CHURCH PRAYER LEADER

Qualifications:
1. Be a mature Christian believer
2. Be a person of prayer
3. Be supportive of the pastor and the church's general direction
4. Have a servant's heart
5. Be a team player

Responsibilities:
1. Lead the church to develop an overall prayer strategy
2. Develop a prayer training program
3. Enlist and train intercessory prayer partners for the staff
4. Oversee the prayer ministry budget and calendar
5. Plan and organize annual prayer emphases in the church
6. Oversee an annual evaluation of the church's prayer ministry
7. Serve as a member of the church council
8. Serve as the church's representative and liaison to other prayer ministries in the community

Term of service:
One year terms, eligible for re-election

Reports to: Senior Pastor

The best way to enlist a prayer coordinator is to look for a church member who already has a passion for prayer. Look where God is already working, and utilize one of the prayer warriors He has given you. If you are not certain who those warriors may be, pray about it!

God will (in the words of the prayer coordinator of Rick Fisher's church) "appoint someone who has a heart for a certain area of prayer to coordinate that ministry of prayer."[10]

3. The Church Should Develop an Overall Strategy For Producing Prayer Warriors

In my little prayer manual, *Serving in Your Church Prayer Ministry,* I have suggested a four-pronged approach to producing prayer warriors.[11] This model is based on Jesus' methods for training and equipping His disciples. Jesus *expected* much from His disciples (Matt. 8:34), *taught* them (Matt. 5-7), *involved* them in ministry (Luke 10:1-16), and built a *relationship* with them (John 15:9-12).

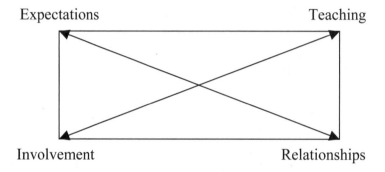

Expectations   Teaching

Involvement   Relationships

Expectations. *Expect* your church members to pray by including prayer in your church covenant, teaching prayer in your new members class, and raising the significance of prayer in your corporate worship services. Sponsor annual prayer training events. Show your church that prayer is mandatory—not optional—in the Christian life.

Teaching. *Teach* the church about prayer through a sermon series on prayer, studies on prayer warriors in the Bible, or other study courses on prayer. Read together the biographies of great prayer warriors. Lead your church to become a college of prayer that produces trained intercessors.

Relationships. Luke 11:1 tells us that Jesus' disciples saw Him pray and then longed to learn to pray as He did. Jesus didn't just teach them about prayer—He lived prayer in front of them. Guide your church to teach prayer *in the context of relationships*. Train parents to teach children to pray. Equip mentors to teach others to pray. Utilize prayer partners and prayer triplets built around established relationships.

Involvement. Work to get members personally involved in the prayer ministry. Set goals for the percentage of active members you want involved. Personally recruit prayer partners. Provide multiple opportunities for members to be a part of the prayer ministry team. Enlist excellent teachers who train potential prayer warriors. Expect your church members to get involved, and then recruit them!

Here's the point of this principle: a prayer-focused pastor and a passionate prayer coordinator still need a strategy to grow a prayer driven church. Passion without direction will not take the church very far.

Application: Prayer and the Vision Cycle

A basic thesis of this book is that moving along the vision cycle usually requires a change of attitude rather than a change of structure. The church must move from an inward focus to an outward one by directing its energies and resources beyond its walls.

That outward focus can begin with the prayer ministry. The rest of this chapter offers ways to use prayer to develop an outreach and ministry mindset.

1. Prayerwalk your community. "Prayerwalking" is exactly what you might expect—believers praying as they walk through a community. The goal of prayerwalking is to "pray onsite with insight," that is, to pray with more focus and intensity because you've seen the needs of the community.[12]

Think about what you might learn about your neighborhood if you take the time to walk, watch, and pray. One New Jersey pastor told me that he did not realize the growth of New Age bookstores in his community until he walked his streets. In response, his church developed a training program to teach their members how to evangelize New Agers. This pastor did not know then about the vision cycle, but his prayerwalking had moved his church toward an outward focus.

Follow these steps to lead your church in prayerwalking:
- ✓ Determine the area to walk (a subdivision, an apartment complex, etc.).
- ✓ Enlist prayerwalkers. Invite everyone—any believer can prayerwalk.
- ✓ As you walk, keep your eyes and ears open to needs in the community.
- ✓ Share your faith if an opportunity arises during the walk.
- ✓ Develop appropriate *outwardly focused* ministries in response to what you learn on the prayerwalk.

2. Offer prayer in your community. I recently read an article about churches in New York City that had established "prayer stations" on the streets of the city. Believers offered prayer for anyone who stopped at the station. To the surprise of the skeptics, the prayer warriors stayed busy. Prayer, it seems, is important to many people. Perhaps your church has an opportunity to set up prayer stations at a local mall, a park, or at a community festival.

Another option is to conduct a prayer survey in the community. Go door-to-door, asking your neighbors this important question: "We're from _____ Church, and we're praying for our community. Do you have any needs we might include on our prayer list?" Record the information, and follow up as needed.

A third possibility is to place "prayer request boxes" at community businesses, as Valley View Church in our city of Louisville does. Business employees and customers write prayer concerns, and Valley View members collect the requests, pray over them, and follow-up. Churches like Valley View—that intentionally offer prayer in their community—think beyond themselves.

3. Establish "lighthouses of prayer" in the neighborhoods around your church. A lighthouse of prayer is a "gathering of two or more people in Jesus' name for the purpose of praying for, caring for, and sharing Christ with their neighbors and others in their sphere of influence."[13] Christians *pray* for their neighbors by name, *care* for them through ministry, and *share* Jesus with them.

My wife and I recently moved into a new home in a newer

subdivision. All of our closest neighbors have moved in since we did, and Pam and I know that God has placed us here to be witnesses for Him. Our outreach has begun by praying for opportunities to get to know these neighbors.

Here's an option for your church. Purchase a map of your community, and pinpoint where your active members live. Encourage them to establish a "lighthouse of prayer" in their areas. Even a simple map can help your church think outwardly.

Through these individual lighthouses praying for neighbors, saturate your community with prayer. Pray for:

✓ opportunities to get to know your neighbors better

✓ wisdom to recognize their needs

✓ resources to help meet those needs

✓ boldness to share Jesus with them

4. Pray for specific groups of people in your community. Few of us will ever forget the tragic events of September 11, 2001. Nor will we forget the bravery of the New York police and firemen who gave their lives trying to rescue others. For weeks, we prayed for these heroes and their families.

Regrettably, it took a tragedy for us to focus our praying on community leaders—leaders who deserved our prayers long before the World Trade Center tragedy. Who are the particular people in your city for whom your church might pray?

Think about all the possibilities. Government leaders. Schoolteachers. Newscasters. Sports figures. Bankers. Factory workers. Garbage collectors. Soldiers. Store clerks. Bus drivers. Musicians. Physicians and nurses. Students . . . and on and on the possibilities go.

Perhaps your church can plan to pray for a different group each quarter. Pray for them, invite them to a special recognition worship service, and welcome them to your church. Your church will focus beyond themselves . . . one group at a time.

Another possibility is to complete a demographic study of your community and to pray for particular groups indicated by that study. For example, your city may have a large number of single or senior adults. There may be a significant percentage of ethnics in your region. Look outward. Find out who lives in your area and pray for them.

5. Pray for one another to be witnesses for Christ. The apostle Paul was one of the greatest missionaries who ever lived. Yet, even he knew that he needed prayer support as he evangelized. Read these words he wrote to the believers in the areas of Ephesus and Colosse:

> And pray on my behalf, that utterance may be given to me in the opening of my mouth, to make known with boldness the mystery of the gospel . . . that in proclaiming it, I may speak boldly, as I ought.
>
> Eph. 6:19-20 (NAS)

> Devote yourselves to prayer . . . praying at the same time for us as well, that God will open up to us a door for the word . . . that I may make it clear in the way I ought to speak.   Col. 4:2-4 (NAS)

Paul did not want to miss an opportunity to share the gospel. He so loved the people outside the church that he prayed for boldness, open doors, and clarity in his presentation. Do you suppose it would be difficult to turn inward if someone were daily praying these prayers for you? What might happen in a church if all of the leaders were praying these prayers for each other?

If you are a pastor, how might your own personal evangelism change if your church prayed this way for you? Probably, your church would take a step in the right direction on the vision cycle. Begin this process by enlisting some prayer partners to pray these texts for you.

6. Pray for missionaries and unreached people groups. Are you aware that 1.7 billion people in the world have little or no access to the gospel? Do you know missionaries who are risking their lives to share the gospel? Are you praying both for the billions held in darkness and for those who are trying to get the gospel to them? Is your church praying for them?

Julie (not her real name) is a missionary serving in the Middle East. She has served in her country for almost ten years, but to her knowledge, no one has yet followed Christ. Still, Julie presses on,

96

loving her people group and praying daily for someone to become a believer.

When I pray for Julie and her work, I can't help but think beyond myself. My heart breaks for a people held in bondage and a missionary who is giving her life to them. That's what happens when you really start praying for missionaries and unreached people groups—your focus shifts away from yourself.

I trust that your church or denomination supports missionary work around the world. Teach your church about this work. Pray intentionally for unreached people groups and missionaries. Doing so will direct your church's focus outwardly.

7. Prayerfully guard against an inward focus. Prayer is a means by which your church can move out of an organizational rut, and it is also a way to guard against falling into the rut again. Almost inevitably, our churches turn inward as they age. Only through the power of God can we help them keep their focus where it belongs: on Him and others.

Gather a group of prayer warriors who will pray daily for your church to see others as Jesus sees them:

> Seeing the people, He felt compassion for them,
> because they were distressed and dispirited like sheep
> without a shepherd. (Matt. 9:36, NAS)

Enlist this group, equip them to pray, and challenge them to hold the church accountable to an outward focused, Great Commission ministry. Make adjustments in your church as necessary to maintain an outward focus. Don't let the elephant get too big.

It All Begins with You

I would not be writing this chapter had it not been for the grace of God and the obedience of a twelve year old believer who shared Christ with me many years ago. My seventh-grade friend, Randy, faithfully obeyed God's call to tell me about Jesus. He told me about Christ's dying for me, and he prayed that God would save me. In fact, he prayed for me for many months before I followed Christ.

One person focused on God first and then on me, and my life has never been the same. How grateful I am for God's willingness to use Randy in my life!

If you want your church to be outward-focused, the process starts with you. You may be only one person, but God works through individuals like you.

Begin now with prayer. Ask Him to give you His eyes for your neighbors and the world.

NOTES

1. Charles Spurgeon, *The Power of Prayer in a Believer's Life* (Lynnwood, WA: Emerald Books, 1993), 105.

2. Thom S. Rainer, *Effective Evangelistic Churches* (Nashville: Broadman and Holman, 1995), 65-80.

3. Henry Blackaby and Claude V. King, *Experiencing God* (Nashville: Broadman and Holman, 1994), 220.

4. Elmer Towns, C. Peter Wagner, and Thom S. Rainer, *The Everychurch Guide to Growth* (Nashville: Broadman and Holman, 1998), 102.

5. Alan Nelson and Gene Appel, *How to Change Your Church without Killing It* (Nashville: Word, 2000), 184-185.

6. Charles Lawless, *Serving in Your Church Prayer Ministry* (Grand Rapids: Zondervan, 2003); Chuck Lawless, *Discipled Warriors* (Grand Rapids: Kregel, 2002).

7. Glen Martin and Dian Ginter, *Power House* (Nashville: Broadman and Holman, 1994), 45.

8. C. Peter Wagner, *Praying with Power* (Ventura: Regal, 1997), 147.

9. Rick Fisher, personal correspondence, March 2003.

10. Ibid.

11. See *Serving in Your Church Prayer Ministry* for a much more complete discussion of this strategy.

12. Steve Hawthorne and Graham Kendrick, *Prayerwalking* (Orlando: Creation House, 1993), 15.

13. Paul A. Cedar, "The Lighthouse Movement," *Pray!* 15 (Nov/Dec 1999): 18.

PART II

LESSONS FROM TRADITIONAL CHURCHES

The following three stories of churches are based on a composite of several churches we have studied. The story of Buck Run Baptist Church, however, is the actual story of one extraordinary church. We pray that you will benefit from the stories of their victories and struggles.

CHAPTER 6

A CHURCH NAMED CALVARY, A PASTOR NAMED JOHN CALVARY COMMUNITY CHURCH

"In his heart
a man plans his course,
but the Lord determines his steps."
Proverbs 16:9

The young minister should have been nervous considering the circumstances. He was a fresh graduate of seminary. Though he had many opportunities to preach over the past several years, this opportunity was a first. He was preaching before a church that could become his first pastorate. A preacher and revivalist to this point, the young man was looking at some 120 people for whom he might be their shepherd.

Most of us would have some level of anxiety. John Morella, however, felt differently. The new year had brought the thirty-two-year-old a fresh opportunity. With seminary behind him, he could invest his life in the lives of God's people. His first emotion was naturally excitement. But on that Sunday morning in January, the emotion changed to a deep empathy of hurt and love for the people he saw.

It was minutes before his appointed moment to preach. Introductions had been made and the congregation awaited the "trial sermon" with anticipation. John was certainly prepared. The sermon he had for the people was not a new one, but it was one of his best. Preachers often refer to such sermons as their "sugar stick." Through the faces of then unnamed individuals in the congregation, God spoke to the young

101

minister. John knew that he could not preach the planned message.

He saw on the faces hurt and sadness. The abundant life seemed to be gone from many. *These people,* John thought, *need love and encouragement.* But he did not have such a sermon at his disposal. What could he do?

John approached the pulpit and paused. Once more the faces spoke volumes in their hurt. The neatly planned notes for that terrific message had been set aside. The pastor-to-be of Calvary Community Church spoke softly. "In the last several minutes God has been speaking to me. I do not have his permission to preach the planned sermon. In fact, I will not preach a sermon as such at all. I want to share with you my testimony."

An uneasy quiet settled over the congregation. This procedure did not fit the rules of calling a pastor, but the people sensed in this young man an honesty and openness that was new to them. So they waited and listened.

John shared with the church the not-so-uncommon testimony of being raised in a Christian home and accepting Christ as a child. But the next words jolted the people to the edge of their pews. "Yes, I had all the advantages a boy could ask for. But I later rebelled and strayed. And in my early adult years I became dependent on drugs. I would sink lower than I ever dreamed possible."

John then shared the deterioration that came to his life, the fleeting thoughts of wondering if life was worth living. In humiliating detail, he told them the true story of a modern-day prodigal. John concluded by sharing with the church that morning when he found himself face down on his mobile home floor, the recipe of alcohol and drugs having done their work the night before. And he told them how he cried out to God to deliver him or kill him. He could no longer live the life of addiction and rebellion. Then, God heard John Morella's prayers. And God answered them gloriously. The grace of God had been more than sufficient.

With the testimony ended, John once again looked into the hurting eyes. He spoke softly once more: "If my Lord can deliver me and, by His grace, allow me to stand before you this morning, then He can bring to your life healing for your hurts and hope for your hopelessness. Will you yield to Him so that He might have His own way in your life?"

The service would conclude with its traditional public invitation, but this one would be different. Barriers were breaking. Strongholds were defeated, and people responded. Something great had happened at Calvary Community Church that January morning. Many more miracles were yet to come.

A Church Named Calvary

You would have to know about Calvary and intentionally take two out-of-the-way turns to find the church in the small Western town. Calvary, at least in its appearance, is the stereotypical traditional church. Hidden in an aging subdivision, there is little about the building that catches one's eye. But the building is not the church; the people are. And that is where the excitement resides.

The year that John came to the church should have been one of excitement for Calvary. The church would soon be celebrating its thirtieth anniversary. The dreams of an earlier generation for a new church in town had become a reality, but the excitement just was not there. John Morella saw it in their faces in January.

The statistics reflected the discouragement of the people. Sunday School attendance had fallen to 111 the previous year, a five-year low for the church. The church had added twenty-five new Sunday School members, but had lost forty-three members. For the first time in years, the nominal increases had reversed to losses. With budget receipts falling from the previous year, Calvary's leaders knew that finding a pastor with significant experience was unlikely. They turned to the resumes of graduating seniors at seminaries. And that is where they came across the name of John Morella.

Calvary Community has since seen steady growth that can best be described as phenomenal in the hindsight of the past six years. The following statistics tell part of the story:

YEAR	1	2	3	4	5	6
Resident Membership	366	390	456	550	600	646
Sunday School Enrollment	289	297	333	461	564	496
Sunday School Attendance	111	118	144	172	190	196
New Members	22	47	78	120	74	69
Baptisms	10	18	42	68	41	36
Total Receipts ($000)	137	108	160	240	218	236

The statistical story is of the six years of John Morella's ministry at Calvary. Sunday School attendance, for example, has increased nearly 100 percent! If you examine the year-by-year data, the church seems healthy rather than miraculous. It takes the vantage point of six years to see the full picture of God's work.

Such is one of the primary points I hope you retain about Calvary and all the examples mentioned in this book. Most traditional churches can grow and do wonderful ministry, but the pace from the inside may seem slower than a snail's pace! Yet, for most traditional churches, the pace of growth like Calvary's is the healthiest. The church can best assimilate the new people and adapt to the changes.

Victories at Calvary

Many church growth experts would have studied Calvary and recommended either relocation or massive renovation of the building. The church has done neither, although some improvements have been made in the physical facilities. What are some key elements in the success story of this traditional church?

A Renewed Attitude

The apostle Paul instructed the beloved Philippian church as follows: "Finally, brothers, whatever is true, whatever is noble, whatever is right, whatever is pure, whatever is lovely, whatever is admirable—if anything is excellent or praiseworthy—*think* about such things" (Phil. 4:8, emphasis added). The apostle knew the possibilities were unlimited for the little church if they kept their minds focused on the matters of God.

Over the past several years, the attitude of Calvary has become increasingly positive. The church is united, moving forward with faith-like optimism. The people are majoring on majors and minoring on minors.

A Deeper Walk

The statistics reflect the outward focus and evangelistic emphasis of Calvary. The church, however, is more than numbers and additions. There seems to be a hunger for a closer walk with Christ, a deeper level of commitment. A prayer ministry led by John's wife has reached many in the church. Answered prayers have become increasingly evident. The phrase "Lordship of Christ" has become more than mere words. It is practiced by numerous members of the church.

Servanthood and Followship

Though John Morella would hardly embrace the authoritarian model of leadership, he is a strong and committed leader. He does not shy away from expressing a clear direction for the church.

But the best of leaders need followers. The people of Calvary have recognized in their pastor his God-given call to be their leader. The church members therefore have a spirit of followship and servanthood.

Souls Won to Christ

During Pastor Morella's ministry at Calvary, over 250 souls have been won to Christ. For a medium-sized church such as Calvary, this number is amazing. The pastor himself has an evangelistic zeal, but such enthusiasm is not limited to him. Numerous laypersons have become soul winners and have developed relationships with unbelievers. A significant number of the decisions for Christ have come from the pool of people commonly described as unchurched. A traditional church has become a dynamic witness for the kingdom!

No evangelistic program per se has played a role in the successful outreach of Calvary. Most of the people won to Christ have come to the church as the result of the enthusiastic testimonies of the members. Though the magnitude is certainly different, the church's evangelistic "methodology" is reminiscent of the first church in Jerusalem. "They broke bread in their homes and ate together with glad and sincere hearts, praising God and enjoying the favor of all the people. And the Lord added to their number daily those who were being saved" (Acts 2:46-47).

The Leadership Style of John Morella

John Morella came to Calvary Community Church with a seminary degree but little or no training in leadership skills. He admits that his first few months of ministry were a time of instinct or, better stated, a true dependence upon the Holy Spirit.

The Issue of Tenure

The pastor's first step was to settle within himself and with God that he was committed to stay at Calvary. Larger churches and greener pastures would tempt him, but he determined to stay until God gave an unmistakably clear call to move. Indeed, opportunities would soon become available, but John refused to discuss such moves. God was simply not in it.

Indeed you will find in each of the three examples in this book that characteristic of the pastor/leader. I have yet to find a traditional church with long-term sustained growth without a pastor who has made a long-term commitment to stay. The pastor of a traditional church must view the progress of the church in five-year increments. Depending upon overnight or one-year successes can be frustrating. A long-term pastorate is a must!

Elephant-Eating Leadership Style

The next move of Pastor Morella was to begin leading the church in small but significant changes. He explains: "The church needed a new vision and new life. I did not decree that certain changes must take place. But I did lead the people to do some things differently. They needed a fresh start and a new perspective."

Some of the changes were mild modifications of the worship services. The lifelessness of the services was reversed with energetic preaching and lively choruses. The aging electronic organ was locked up indefinitely. John's wife contributed her talents on the piano. A spirit of celebration became the norm at Calvary.

Have Calvary's worship services become truly contemporary? Hardly. I have been present at several of their services and testify that there is much that is traditional about them. The difference is not so much the style of worship as it is the spirit of worship. The enthusiasm is contagious and the good news is really good news.

The new spirit of the worship services is the result of both planned changes and an openness to God's Spirit. Because a true dependence on God and the power of prayer exists at Calvary, the services become a time of anticipation. One can sense God's power simply by walking into the sanctuary.

For example, John led Calvary to hold a revival service. God began doing many great things over this five-day period. One morning, after one of those revival services, two men walked into the sanctuary to deliver a newly-donated grand piano. One of the workers literally froze in his tracks and exclaimed, "God is here!" He fell to his knees and began praying. Now that is revival!

Other changes began to take place at a methodical pace. The pastor preached and pleaded for lost souls, and the people caught the vision. They no longer looked inward; their focus was outward. Slowly, more laypersons began to come forward to be involved in ministry. The church was becoming a New Testament church. Fellowship groups formed in homes. Sunday School, however, was not replaced with home cell groups. To the contrary, the statistics seem to indicate that the fellowship groups strengthened Sunday School.

John Morella credits a core group of leaders, particularly the search committee who presented him to the church, for their willingness to follow his leadership. "They did not have to accept me and my suggestions," John stated. "But some of the dedicated leaders in the church had a humility about themselves and a willingness to be led."

While the pastor points to the people for many of Calvary's successes, the church members credit John and his Christ-like dedication for leading the church to new heights. One long-time member put it this way: "I am so glad that God sent us a human being as a pastor, a leader who recognizes his own humanity and vulnerability."

From the perspective of leadership ability, we could summarize the strengths of John Morella into five basic areas. By all means, the first characteristic would be the most important.

Dependence on God. As I spoke with members of Calvary, their assessment of their pastor came in different but similar words. "He recognizes his own imperfections." All of the comments pointed to a dependence on God. Pastor Morella is receptive to any of the latest methodologies, but he recognizes that true growth can only come from the sovereign God.

He recognized that this dependence upon what he believed was a difficult lesson for him. The pastor was debating on how to handle the crowded Sunday School conditions that had developed with the consistent growth of the church. The classic church growth response was multiple Sunday Schools. All of the organizational and methodological principles pointed to this solution. John Morella proceeded with this plan despite his own uneasiness.

After the dual Sunday School was implemented, the spirit of the church suffered. All of the literature had offered this alternative, but it just was not working at Calvary. John recognized that he had allowed the church to move ahead of God's plan. He soon reversed his own decision and returned to one Sunday School.

Many pastors would have had difficulty reversing themselves on such a major move. Calvary's willingness to do so is a tribute both to a pastor whose ego was in God's control, and to a church who was willing to follow their leader in and out of a major decision.

A Commitment to Stay. Other churches would soon note the excitement at Calvary. Word would travel from church to church. Eventually, another church would be knocking on the pastor's door. But John Morella refused to move because God had not given him such leadership or permission.

It has been my experience in consulting with hundreds of traditional churches around the nation that the most productive years of a pastor's ministry begin after he completes five years of service. That is not to say that victories will be scarce the first five years. To the contrary, major victories are possible. But those victories will fade quickly if the pastoral turnover is high. Long-lived successes require long-term pastorates.

Wisdom in Initiating Change. This book has been repetitious for a reason. One of the major reasons so many traditional churches are plateaued or declining is weak leadership that either moves too quickly or hardly at all. If no change takes place, the church begins to look inward and becomes introspective. A maintenance mentality permeates all the ministries of the church. On the other hand, a rapid infusion of change can create divisiveness and fear.

The changes that have taken place at Calvary have been initiated with wisdom most of the time. The people have been able to adjust to each new change and even to anticipate more exciting ventures. Ironically, in an interview with John Morella, he commented on the snail's-pace change which was taking place in the church. When I gave him a five-year perspective, however, he was amazed at all of the new developments in the church. Leaders often need to step back and see their churches from an outsider's perspective. The view can be enlightening.

An Attitude of Encouragement. Recent church growth literature has flooded the book market with cries for churches to be "user friendly." The material is well-intentioned. We in churches must be sensitive to the needs of those who are lost and unchurched. The problem, however, is that many churches have taken these suggestions to extremes. Basic Christian doctrines such as sin, hell, and God's justice have all but disappeared in some churches. Is it possible to be balanced biblically, yet offer encouragement to our people? The leadership style of Pastor Morella would give us a good example of a positive answer to this question.

John does not shy away from any of the difficult and hard-hitting doctrines of Scripture. You know there is no element of compromise after listening to one of his sermons. But the pastor consistently presents the truth in love. Messages of chastisement are more than balanced with messages of encouragement. John's interaction with the people of Calvary in counseling and in informal conversations is consistently a time of encouragement.

Such an attitude of encouragement must be genuine, not contrived. How can we as leaders offer consistent encouragement to the people in our churches? That answer can be found in the fifth and final assessment of Pastor Morella's leadership style.

A Love for the People. It has been my impression that Calvary Community Church accepts John Morella and his leadership, strengths and flaws, because they know he loves them. From the first day he came to Calvary, his heart has hurt for their hurts and rejoiced in their joys. Such a love can only come from a right relationship with Christ. Once we truly realize how our Savior loves us unconditionally, we can then love God's children just as they are. "This is the message you heard from the beginning: We should love one another. . . . This is how we know what love is: Jesus Christ laid down his life for us. And we ought to lay down our lives for our brothers" (1 John 3:11, 16).

Struggles at Calvary

Calvary Community Church has grown significantly over the past several years. To view their story from a distance gives the appearance of uninterrupted growth with no problems. But Calvary is a church of sinful humans, just like mine or yours. Neither their leader nor the people themselves are perfect. Let us see some of the struggles that have accompanied the growth.

The Need for Stronger Lay Leadership

On the one hand, many of the members of Calvary have stepped forward to provide leadership in key positions. On the other hand, much of the ministry is still done by the pastor. For example, the hospital visitation ministry is a very time-consuming process, and the majority of the members have the expectation that the pastor should be the key minister in this area. Unfortunately, many of the members spend their hospital stays in towns other than the church's community. It is not unusual for Pastor Morella to make visits some three hours away. One visit can thus consume an entire day's time.

While no pastor should ever cease making hospital visits, the burden of this ministry at Calvary and other churches should be carried by the laity of the church. Remember Paul's instructions to the church at Ephesus? "It was he who gave some to be . . . pastors and teachers, to prepare God's people for works of service, so that the body of Christ may be built up" (Eph. 4:11-12). Until the church grasps the God-given call of the laity to do ministry, the body of Christ, the local church, will never be completely in sync with God's plan.

At Calvary, like the vast majority of churches in America, the mindset is still prevalent that the pastor (and other staff) is hired to do all the ministry in the church. However, the pastor's primary roles are equipping (Eph. 4:11-12), prayer, and ministry of the Word (Acts 6:3-4).

Struggles in Holding Gains

Over a five-year period, Calvary welcomed 388 new members, a remarkable number for an established mid-sized church in an established neighborhood. Sunday School attendance, however, increased by only seventy-eight in that same period. In other words, about 20 percent of the new members would be present on a given Sunday five years later. One of three reasons could explain this phenomenon: (1) loss of significant numbers of members which have offset the gains; (2) reduced participation by existing members; or (3) reduced participation by new members. Since Calvary has lost relatively few members, a combination of the latter two reasons seems to explain the low assimilation rate.

What would be a healthy goal for Calvary? If 40 percent of all new members were present in Sunday School five years later, the church could feel a healthy sense of pride in its accomplishment. How that could be accomplished is the subject of the next struggle.

Organizational Struggles

When I speak of organizational struggles in a church, I refer primarily to the Sunday School, the key small group in most churches. At Calvary the Sunday School organization is augmented by home fellowship groups. Pastor Morella saw the need for more intensive care than is usually provided by Sunday School classes. The small groups have not accomplished all that they were envisioned to do. The original idea was that the first eight groups would expand to eventually cover most of the church membership. Though some of the groups are strong, the number of the home fellowships has decreased from eight to five. Thus only a small portion of the church is active in the small groups.

The responsibility of small-group assimilation and discipleship is thus still primarily in the hands of the Sunday School leaders. In some of the Sunday School classes, ministry is ongoing and active. In others some inactive members have not been contacted for months. Like all churches that depend on Sunday School as the primary assimilation arm of the church, a system of accountability for ministry and outreach must exist at all levels of the organization.

It has been noted in many church growth books that the worship service is the primary "front door" or entry point for prospective members today. I would add relationships plus the worship service are the two entry points in the church. The tasks of Sunday School today are largely assimilation and discipleship. If we are to conserve the gains with which God has blessed us, we need a dynamic small-group organization (such as Sunday School) that cares for, disciples, and ministers to the people. Such is the challenge for Calvary and many other churches in America today.

Calvary on the Vision Cycle

Though the leadership of Calvary has not had the illustrative device of a vision cycle to assist it in the growth process, the church has followed many of its principles. Let us revisit the vision cycle to understand Calvary's growth.

Pastor Morella began his ministry with wisdom. The organization and worship of Calvary was anemic when he arrived. Rather than try to reinvent the organizations, as many new pastors are apt to do, he refocused the church on reaching people for Christ and doing ministry. He changed the focus from introspective to outward. His preaching and emphases on outreach caused the people to look beyond themselves (step 1 on the vision cycle).

Many of the people of Calvary then began doing ministry as they looked outward and answered their God-given call (step 2). The prayer ministry is one example of the laity unleashed. John Morella would like to see more lay leadership rise up and initiate and lead ministries. While the church admittedly has not been fully unleashed, significant progress has been made.

With the church looking outward and leading in ministries, Pastor Morella has been able to show the church members the possibilities for reaching the town (step 3). Such a vision would have accomplished little when he first arrived. The people had to look outward and do ministry before the vision made sense. Now there exists excitement and anticipation about God's work in their community.

3: *Rekindling the Vision*
● seeing the possibilities to reach Braswell

2: *Unleashing the Church*
● "permission" to do ministry
● prayer ministry

4: *Ministry and Growth*
● new ministries
● nearly 100% increase in attendance

VISION CYCLE

Calvary Community Church

1: *Outward Focus*
● evangelistic/outreach preaching
● renewal of attitudes
● outreach emphasis

5: *Organization and Structure*
● THE CHALLENGE TODAY

Ministry and growth are natural consequences of the preceding points on the vision cycle (step 4). The church's nearly doubling in attendance in five years is but one outgrowth of the excitement at Calvary. The reputation of the church is penetrating the community and beyond.

The challenge today for Calvary is the structuring of an organization that will assimilate the new members coming into the church weekly (step 5). At Calvary the likelihood is that the Sunday School will be such an organization. Every class should be tightly organized with outreach leaders, care group leaders, and caring teachers. Goals for growth and ministry can be established. Each class should seek ways to start "daughter" classes so that future growth can be handled in smaller groups. A system of accountability needs to be in place to assure that all of this restructuring takes place.

A Church Named Calvary, A Pastor Named John

Calvary Community Church is more than a pastor. The fire of the Holy Spirit burns in the hearts of hundreds. Yet Calvary is a traditional church in an older neighborhood. It defies church growth prognostications with its building and location.

A pastor named John Morella saw the possibilities that God had for Calvary. He loved the people, ministered to the people, and challenged the people. He hung in there in good times and challenging times. He made a commitment to stay.

According to all the data I have, almost 90 percent of the churches of Calvary's size and demographic situation are declining. Yet here is a church that has doubled its attendance in five years. For you pastors and church leaders who are discouraged about your present situation, take heart from the example of Calvary. Your church's turnaround may take five, eight, ten years, or more. But hang in there. It is happening at Calvary Community Church. And it can happen at your church.

CHAPTER 7

THE MIRACLE CALLED BUCK
RUN BUCK RUN BAPTIST CHURCH, FRANKFORT, KENTUCKY

"Everyone was filled with awe, and many wonders and
miraculous signs were done by the apostles."

Acts 2:43

If ever there existed a stereotypical traditional church, Buck Run
Baptist Church would have fit that mold. Begun in 1818 as the result of
a revival, the church was founded by John Taylor, a famous pioneer
preacher of that day. Taylor, considered by some church historians to
be a pivotal religious figure of the nineteenth century, had started a
church in Frankfort a year earlier. The fiery preacher, however, was
more suited for the country life of Buck Run, where his ministry would
continue for seven years.

Buck Run would have a succession of outstanding ministers to lead
the church. Among them were J. M. Frost, founder of The Sunday
School Board of the Southern Baptist Convention; F. W. Eberhart,
president of Georgetown College; Robert Culpepper and Bryant Hicks,
two notable leaders in the foreign mission enterprise of the Southern
Baptist Convention; and Peter Pentz, who would become the pastor of
the largest church in South Africa and president of his denomination's
convention.

Perhaps the most exciting favorite son of Buck Run was George
Dupee, an African-American who was born into slavery. Dupee was
raised in the church as a member and often preached for the mainly
white congregation. He was licensed to preach in 1846 and ordained to
the gospel ministry by the church in 1851. After being granted his
freedom, Dupee left Buck Run to found fourteen black congregations.
He baptized over seven thousand new Christians and organized the first

state-wide Baptist association for black churches in Kentucky. He served as its moderator for twenty-eight consecutive years.

While Buck Run impacted the kingdom with its influential leaders, its influence in its own community was less than dramatic. Admittedly, the community surrounding the church has remained small. But three traumatic divisions in the church have stopped would-be growth over the course of a century.

As a result of these schisms, two other churches were started: Providence Church in 1857 and Calvary Church in 1948. The adoption of a church constitution and the establishment of a deacon rotation system saw Buck Run lose half of its members in 1960.

In 1966 Robert H. Jackson, a student at The Southern Baptist Theological Seminary in Louisville, became pastor. The building by that time had deteriorated. Only four small Sunday School rooms were available for use and the church budget had declined to $10,000.

Pastor Jackson would stay with the church for eight years, after which he sensed God's call to become pastor of the First Baptist Church in Monroeville, Alabama. The legacy that Robert left Buck Run was a strong church averaging 175 in attendance, a healthy budget with a surplus in the treasury, and a new parsonage for future pastors. When Bob Jackson left Buck Run in 1974 he thought that chapter of his life had come to a close. Little did he know then that the God of miracles had other plans.

God Is Not Done with You Yet!

Some of you readers may be a discouraged pastors or staff members in your church. You have tried everything you know to lead your church in new ministries and growth. You may even be wondering if God's hand is off your ministry.

May the story that you will read about Bob Jackson be a source of strength and encouragement to you. May you realize that the same God of miracles in the Old and New Testament is still working miracles today. And may you understand clearly that God is not done with you yet!

The Early Years at Monroeville

Robert Jackson was the successful pastor of the First Baptist Church of Monroeville from 1974 to 1981. Attendance doubled and the budget increased likewise. But Bob discovered something about his ministry that made him uncomfortable. "I could make things happen," he said, "but, for the most part, God was not in it." Nevertheless, he pushed himself both day and night to be successful. As his ministry came to a close in Monroeville, he discovered that he had become an emotional, physical, and spiritual wreck.

Pastor Jackson realized that the power of the living God was missing in his life. He subsequently gave prayer a place of priority on his calendar. He read the Bible for his own benefit, not just for sermon preparation. And he read inspirational books, one of which was Ray Ortlund's *Lord, Make My Life a Miracle.* He devoured the book and came to realize that he needed to give himself totally to Christ, to submit to the Lord for a Spirit-filled life. That night, on his knees in prayer, he asked the Lord to "make his life a miracle." He further prayed, "And God, I will pay whatever price it takes for that to become a reality." Such a prayer was dangerous, because God decided to answer it.

From Alabama to Mississippi

Within a few weeks of this prayer, Pastor Jackson was called to become pastor of the First Baptist Church of Brandon, Mississippi. This church was one of the largest churches in the state, located just outside Jackson, the state capital. The adrenaline was flowing again as Robert Jackson considered the prospect of beginning a new ministry in one of the fastest-growing areas in the South.

In his first week of ministry at Brandon, the pastor suffered a massive heart attack. He was only forty-four years old. Robert remained in intensive care, fighting for his life, for a week. After the immediate crisis was over, the physician gave the family the bad news. The damage to the heart was so extensive that nothing surgically could be done. The doctor even suggested that Robert could never resume a full-time ministry.

Nevertheless, the pastor amazed everyone when he resumed preaching in one morning service within four months, two morning services within five months, and the Sunday evening service in six months. As in his other churches, the numerical growth was significant. But something far more significant than numerical successes were taking place in the pastor's life.

The Dark Night of the Soul

Robert continued to be plagued by poor health in his ministry at Brandon. In 1984 he was hospitalized five times in a five-month period. The last hospital stay resulted in a deep depression. The depression was so deep that Bob could neither carry on an extended conversation with his wife nor read a daily newspaper and comprehend it. The pastor still refers to these times as "the dark night of the soul."

Bob soon resigned from the Brandon church. During the depths of his despair, a friend and full-time evangelist, Gary Bowlin, asked to see him. "Brother Bob," he said, "I have a message God asked me to give you. God asked me to tell you that your greatest years of ministry are yet before you!" The former pastor responded, "I accept this word though I do not understand it."

Robert Jackson continued his diligence in prayer, even at times of greatest despair. He also began a vigorous exercise program. Slowly he began to be restored physically and spiritually. His walk with the Lord became, in his words, "Sweeter by far than anything I have ever known."

He began to see changes in his attitude about life, ministry, and his relationship with God. Success was no longer important. Faithfulness was.

Bob began sensing a message from God in April 1990. The message would be repeated numerous times over a five-month period: "Return and build the temple!" At first he was baffled by the seemingly nonsensical message, but then the mandate became clear. He was to return to a former pastorate and lead them in "building the temple." One question remained unanswered. Where would he go? All four of his former churches had pastors with whom they were very happy.

About one week later, it seemed that God's answer had come. The pastor of First Baptist Church in Monroeville had resigned. Some of the church leaders approached their former pastor about returning, promising to add staff so that his load would not be too strenuous.

The possibility made good sense. Bob and his wife had built a new home in Monroeville. He was forty miles from his father who was not in good health, and Bob's wife had recently moved her mother to a retirement apartment in the area.

Despite the seemingly perfect situation, Bob and Gail Jackson could not find peace about returning to First Baptist. They struggled for several months with the decision. Finally, Bob hand-delivered a letter to the chairman of the search committee. He would not accept the call.

Within the next week a call came from the Buck Run Baptist Church in Frankfort, the church he had led while in seminary. The caller was to the point: "Brother Jackson, our church is planning to go into a building program and our pastor has unexpectedly resigned to return to Virginia. Would you consider coming back to lead us again?" The peace that had not been present in the prior decision was immediately evident. Shortly after the call, Bob and Gail Jackson would be returning to Frankfort.

The Miracle Called Buck Run

If you are pastor reading this book, imagine this scenario with me for a moment. A church in a rural area outside of Frankfort, Kentucky, calls you on the telephone. They tell you that their pastor has resigned, and your name has been mentioned as a possible successor. Would you pray about meeting with the search committee?

After the call you begin some preliminary research of the church and its community. You discover that the church is located in a quaint little village called the Forks at Elkhorn. The church building can be found on the banks where the south and north forks of the Elkhorn Creek come together before flowing into the Kentucky River. Your conclusion? Lovely location with limited potential.

You then get some data on the church. The first red flag that hits you is the church's founding date of 1818. Undoubtedly, you think, this church is so steeped in tradition that they will never go anywhere. You then review the statistics of Buck Run. They confirm your worst fears.

Average attendance is 120, less than one person per year of existence. In fact the recent history is even more dismal. Over the past fifteen years the church has declined from 175 in attendance to the present level of 120. Few people have joined the church in recent years.

You conclude that this church is just a few years away from death. There is simply nothing that can be done to prevent the situation. And you forget the possibility of God's power and Jesus' own words when He reminded us: "With man this is impossible, but with God all things are possible" (Matt. 19:26).

The Miracle in Numbers

Statistics do not tell the whole story. They can never replace the testimonies of individuals whose lives have been changed. But the numbers do point to the greater miracle of God's work in a very traditional church.

	YEAR 1	YEAR 4	Increase
Resident Members	388	630	62%
Baptisms	4	44	1,000%
Other New Members	11	80	627%
Total New Members	15	124	727%
Sunday School Enrollment	218	470	116%
Sunday School Average Attendance	122	285	133%
Worship Attendance	120	360	200%
Total Receipts ($000)	$171	$505	196%

The church more than doubled its attendance in three years. That pace of growth in a small church created numerous space problems. Every conceivable part of the building had to be used for education and worship space. A major building program ensued to facilitate present and future growth.

The People Reached by Buck Run

Two-thirds of first-time visitors to Buck Run say they came to the church because they were invited by a church member, or because they came with a friend or spouse. In other words, relationships have been the key impetus for reaching people in the community.

Not surprisingly, the second most frequently cited reason for visitors coming to Buck Run is the reputation of the church. "I heard about the excitement and decided to see what was going on," said one visitor. In many circles Buck Run is the topic of conversation both in the local community and the larger Frankfort area. As a result, one-fourth of all first-time visitors said they came to the church because of the excitement that had been communicated to them.

The two factors bringing first-time visitors cannot be viewed separately. Because of the excitement at Buck Run, members are more likely to invite their friends, neighbors, relatives, or acquaintances. Relationship invitation and excitement build upon one another.

While the surge of visitors has been impressive, the church's ability to retain those visitors has been equally impressive. A high percentage of these people are not only staying, but they are becoming members of the church. Perhaps the most common explanation by recent members for their joining the church could only be stated in spiritual terms. These new members literally felt led by God to join Buck Run. One typical comment was: "The presence of the Lord is felt here." Another stated: "The presence of the Holy Spirit is so evident." Yet another new member said simply, "I feel that the Lord led me here." Others made similar comments about the excitement of the church: "I wanted to be part of a church on fire for the Lord."

The development of relationships before and after joining the church played a major role. Even those who knew no one prior to joining felt like the members of Buck Run were extraordinarily friendly. One out of ten new members said a primary reason for their remaining at the church was its friendliness.

Other important factors have contributed to the dynamic growth of the church. The music ministry and preaching are often cited as such factors by new members. The personalities and unity of the staff are also mentioned.

For you readers who have inundated yourselves with church growth reading over the past several years, you will be interested in noting the factors which did not contribute or played only a minor role in the growth of the church.

For example, new members never mentioned advertising or a marketing strategy as having influenced them to come to the church. Nor did they speak of direct mail or telemarketing as an impetus which brought them to Buck Run. While such marketing tools may have a limited impact in creating an awareness of the church, they are never effective alone. The church and the people must bear testimony to the work of God. Once the people walk in the door, they must know that something special is happening in the house of God.

Another factor not cited in the growth of the church is the style of the worship service. Buck Run mixes with quality the old and the new in their morning worship services. A traditional opening hymn may be followed by praise choruses. Special music may range from gospel quartets to traditional choral arrangements to a contemporary solo to an ageless classical arrangement.

While many church growth advocates point to a particular style of music as a growth factor, the people of Buck Run have responded well to a wide variety of styles In a recent survey, over 98 percent of the congregation said that "the music leadership is one of our greatest assets." The style was not the factor cited, rather the "excellent blend of all types of music, both old and new."

It is my prayer that this story of an established, traditional church will be an encouragement to pastors and other leaders around the nation. The story of Buck Run is not one of methodology, demographics, or a building program. It is the story of God's supernatural work in an unlikely place at an unlikely time; but, then again, surprises seem to be a part of the Master's plan. The God who allowed His Son to be born in a lowly manger is the same God who wants to work miracles in your church today.

The Outreach Plan of Buck Run

It may be stated with certainty that methodologies alone have not built Buck Run Baptist Church. But the leadership of the church has worked cooperatively with a sovereign God to bring forth this harvest. In this section we will examine some ways that such cooperation has taken place.

The Priority of Prayer. The power of prayer is taken seriously at Buck Run. When Pastor Jackson met with the leadership of the church to discuss his returning as pastor, he made this priority clear. In one of his first sermons as the new pastor, Robert Jackson stated: "I come back with no grandiose plans of building a great building or growing a big church. I come back with one agenda: to join with you in making the living presence of our reigning Lord a reality in the life and work of this congregation."

The importance of prayer is evident immediately to the visitor participating in a worship service. Pastor Jackson will call upon those desiring prayer at some point during the service. As all the people join hands, the pastor prays for the needs of the people. Healings of the body, emotions, relationships, and spirit are often testified as a result of this prayer time.

On Saturday mornings an intercessory prayer group called the Eliezer Prayer Fellowship meets at the sanctuary altar. The purpose of this intercession is to pray specifically for the Sunday services. Prayers go forth for the ministers, the musicians, the ushers, and the lost people who may attend. If the intercessors know of unbelievers who may be attending, they are called by name.

Pastor Jackson has at times called the people of Buck Run to a time of prayer and fasting. In March 1993, such a call was made to reach people on Easter. A seemingly impossible goal of 508 for Sunday School was set. The results were phenomenal. On Easter Sunday 520 people attended Sunday School and 640 were present in the two worship services! Remember, Buck Run was a traditional church in an average location with 120 present three years earlier.

The Wednesday night service at Buck Run is called the "Praise and Prayer Service." Members of the church family share in testimony answered prayers from the previous week. It is a time of joy and encouragement. People are drawn to and encouraged by the stories about a God who is still working miracles among His people.

Rob Jackson, son of Robert Jackson, believes that prayer is the key element to Buck Run's growth. "God is doing some unbelievable things at Buck Run because His people are daring to open up the channel for the power of the Spirit to flow. . . . They are paying the price in prayer," said the younger Jackson. He further stated that aggressive advertising is not really necessary "when prayers are being answered supernaturally. Such a church does not have to beat a lot of drums and sound off blaring sirens to get the attention of the community. The word swiftly travels and, as Micah 4:1 states, 'the Lord's temple will be established; . . . and peoples will stream to it.'"

Ministries of Caring. Buck Run Baptist Church offers many ministries that reach out to the community. The people of the church are involved in ministries to nursing homes, jails, and various food ministries. A children's crisis ministry works through the local hospital emergency room to provide four thousand stuffed dolls each year to children experiencing sudden traumas.

Deacons provide communion to homebound Christians. Over one hundred members were involved in building a Habitat for Humanity home for a Haitian refugee family. Each year the church collects from its members tons of clothing for mountain children in eastern Kentucky. Mission teams are sent from the church to help struggling congregations in Indiana. Ministry is ongoing and dynamic.

While all of these ministries may not be directly related to outreach, they are positive influences upon the growth of the church. The community is hearing the unspoken message of Buck Run Baptist Church clearly: the people really do care. Is it then any wonder that more and more people are attracted to this revitalized church?

Traditional Outreach. Buck Run has a traditional night of outreach. Monday evening is set aside to visit prospects, particularly those who visited the previous Sunday. Though such traditional visitation is less effective today in many churches, it still makes a difference at Buck Run. At least 95 percent of all people who joined the church in the past three years were first contacted on Monday night visitation.

The Struggles and the Future

Three primary struggles concern Pastor Jackson. All three factors are symptomatic of growing pains.

The Space Problem

In the first three years of Bob Jackson's tenure at Buck Run, the church was adding slightly more than two members per week. That pace is now almost five new members each week! The dynamic growth of the church has created space problems requiring innovative solutions. Many of these struggles will soon be handled by the new $1.75 million multipurpose facility. In the meantime the church has used closed-circuit television for the 11:00 A.M. worship service, shuttle parking from a body shop, and Sunday School classes in the most unlikely locations.

It is not the space constraints that concern the pastor. They can be solved with innovations and additional facilities. Rather, it is the attitude of a small number of the members who do not attend because they consider the crowds at the church too much of a hassle. A few of the members have expressed their unwillingness to attend the church with its present inconveniences. Although these people represent only a small portion of the total membership, such an attitude of selfishness can be detrimental to any church, especially a church in revival like Buck Run.

The Assimilation Problem

On a given Sunday, at least two-thirds of those in attendance at Buck Run will be relatively new members. These new members are often waiting on longer-term members to help them assimilate into the church. The problem is that there are not enough longer-term members for the newer members! Relationships may not develop easily because of the relatively small base of assimilated members in the church.

For now the drop-out rate is low. Pastor Jackson has done an admirable job of explaining to new members why someone may not be reaching out to them. The church faces the challenge of getting the new members involved in small groups and in ministries. The task may prove to be difficult because of the present workload required just to minister. The members must reach out to those who visit the church. Lay leaders must be equipped as expeditiously as possible to assist the staff in their tremendous responsibilities.

Ministry Needs

The reputation of Buck Run Baptist Church is growing. Numerous communities in the Frankfort area have heard about the church of miracles. Visitors are coming from all directions. And new members are joining despite the long distances they have to drive.

As one might expect, some of those who are coming to Buck Run bring with them tremendous ministry needs. They have problems and concerns and hear about a church that is really making a difference for the kingdom. So they bring their burdens to the church with the hopes that, somehow, God will work a miracle in their lives.

Bob Jackson welcomes such people to Buck Run. After all, the church is called to minister to the world. The church is the body of

Christ (1 Cor. 12:27), and the incarnated Christ clearly met people at their point of need and ministered to them.

The problem, says the pastor, is not the ministry needs per se. Rather it is the expectations in the minds of some that Buck Run Baptist Church will be a "quick-fix" solution to all their problems.

Again, the call is for the leadership to hasten the process of equipping ministry leaders in the church. The reputation of Buck Run will continue to grow. People with needs will continue to flock to the church. The ability of the church to minister to these people will not only help them temporally—it could make a difference eternally.

Buck Run and the Vision Cycle

Buck Run Baptist Church is an ideal example of the vision cycle at work. In the past few years the church has make at least one full cycle. Let us view their progress illustratively:

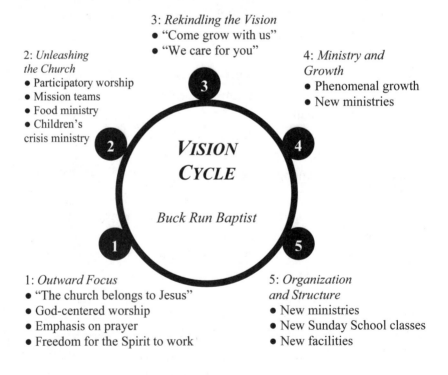

3: *Rekindling the Vision*
- "Come grow with us"
- "We care for you"

2: *Unleashing the Church*
- Participatory worship
- Mission teams
- Food ministry
- Children's crisis ministry

4: *Ministry and Growth*
- Phenomenal growth
- New ministries

VISION CYCLE

Buck Run Baptist

1: *Outward Focus*
- "The church belongs to Jesus"
- God-centered worship
- Emphasis on prayer
- Freedom for the Spirit to work

5: *Organization and Structure*
- New ministries
- New Sunday School classes
- New facilities

Outward Focus

When Bob Jackson was seeking God's will to go to Buck Run, he made two points clear to the church's leadership. First, the church belongs to Jesus. No group, no staff member, no deacon body would control the church. It would be in the hands of Jesus. Second, the Holy Spirit would have freedom to work. The church would let Him guide their decisions and ministries.

By his statements Pastor Jackson was leading Buck Run to the first step away from organizational stagnation. The church immediately became outwardly focused as the people looked to God for a new and fresh direction.

Such an initial step is critical to any church, particularly a traditional church. The people began to look beyond their buildings and organizations. They then began to believe that God could move in new and exciting directions.

Bob Jackson did not attack any organization or structure. He did not mandate that a "sacred" institution had to change. He simply led the people to look beyond the organization to the possibilities of God's work. The outward focus was further enhanced by the worship services which centered around God and His power and holiness. Likewise, Buck Run's emphasis on prayer caused the people to look beyond themselves and to look outward.

Unleashing the Church

As the people of Buck Run began to see the church from God's perspective, they also began to see that the King of kings would use them and work through them. Worship was no longer a spectator event. Mission teams traveled to other states to work with other churches. Helping ministries for children and hurting families began. The church became unleashed by the Spirit to do ministry.

Rekindling the Vision

Though Buck Run is nearly two centuries old, God's vision for the church has not always been evident. Bob Jackson now communicates that vision with slogans like "Come Grow with Us" and "We Care for You." The people of Buck Run and the surrounding communities know that the words are more than mere slogans or marketing tools. They reflect a reality that is sweeping the church: people are being reached for Christ and people are being ministered to in Christ's name.

In 1990, when Bob Jackson first came to Buck Run, the words in the slogans would have had little substance. Now the members of the church understand the truth behind this vision. They understand because they were a part of the vision even before it was articulated.

Ministry and Growth

The ministries and growth that have resulted from God's vision have been nothing short of miraculous. Not only does the growth show few signs of waning, indications are that the growth rate is accelerating.

Organization and Structure

Buck Run is now establishing new organizations to meet the growing ministry needs of the church. New Sunday School classes and ministries are being started on a regular basis. A multipurpose building was completed in 1994 to help meet the growing space demands.

The organization and structure of Buck Run Baptist Church looks almost completely different than it did in 1990. Wisely, the pastor did not attempt to change the structures until the new growth and new ministries demanded the change. The people now view the organizational changes as a positive consequence of all the great things happening at the church.

The Miracle Called Buck Run

In an earlier century the fires of revival swept through the state of Kentucky. Then a frontier state, Kentucky was forever changed by the move of a sovereign God. In a more recent time, a small college called Asbury was touched by fresh wind of the Spirit. Some church historians believe that as many as one million people came to Christ as a result of the Asbury revival of 1970.

Some thirty miles north of Wilmore, the site of the Asbury revival, is the place of yet another move of God in Kentucky. Buck Run Baptist Church, five miles east of Frankfort, has not yet seen what God will ultimately do in their midst.

Growth can come to a church in several ways. Some churches have great demographic potential; other churches may grow due to exciting worship services. Even other churches may have aggressive outreach programs that engender solid growth.

Nothing is wrong with any of these models. Indeed lives can be reached for Christ in all such churches. But ultimately, true revival comes from a sovereign God, not from human efforts. In my humble estimation, that is the story of Buck Run. One servant, open to the work of God, has led an entire congregation to an openness for the hand of God to move upon their church. And God in His sovereignty has brought revival.

If you are struggling, dear friend, hear the story of Buck Run. Hear about a God who chose to move in a most unlikely spot. Fall on your knees that He might send such a revival to your church. I am convinced that our Lord is waiting on many Christian leaders to depend totally upon Him to lead His churches. Remember, Bob Jackson made two simple but profound commitments to God. The church would belong to Jesus, and God's Spirit would have freedom to do His work. Then revival came.

I believe that the promise made to Solomon for Israel is just as valid for our churches today: "If my people, who are called by name, will humble themselves and pray and seek my face and turn from their wicked ways, then will I hear from heaven and will forgive their sin and heal their land" (2 Chron. 7:14).

The miracle is called Buck Run Baptist Church. The next miracle could be your church.

CHAPTER 8

WAITING ON GOD AT EWART FORK EWART FORK CHURCH, EWART FORK, KANSAS

"Yet the Lord longs to be gracious to you;
he rises to show you compassion.
For the Lord is a God of justice.
Blessed are all who wait for him!"

Isaiah 30:18

You have just accepted the call to become the pastor of a church in a community that has a population of less than one thousand. The community is rural. The people of the small town are very close to one another, both in physical proximity and in kindred spirit.

Like any pastor you have high hopes for your church. In the beginning of your ministry, you begin to see some of those hopes realized. Attendance jumps from 189 to 225 and, even more remarkably, total receipts increase from $170,000 to $217,000. You feel affirmed and certain of your call to this church.

Six years go by quickly. The initial burst of growth in your first year of ministry now seems more like a short honeymoon than a long-term trend. In the five years that followed, average attendance plateaued, only 227 compared to 225. And the financial record is more than a small concern. The total receipts for your church have actually declined slightly in the five-year period.

If you were the pastor at this point in the church's history, what would your reaction be? Would you be discouraged? You could look at the church's records and discover that attendance has not really changed. Eleven years, six of which are in your ministry, and the church has shown no growth! What is your response?

From a statistical viewpoint, you should have already gone to another church. After all, six years exceeds the average tenure of pastors, and this church offers little future!

Somewhere between years three and seven of their ministries, a large number of pastors of traditional churches leave for another ministry. And I am convinced that this phenomenon explains to some extent the massive number of declining and plateaued churches in America. Pastors become discouraged at a relatively early time in their ministry. They decide to move to another church, thinking that another place of ministry would be more fruitful.

Yet the empirical evidence, from a variety of different sources, points to the fact that a pastor's most productive years often begin after their seventh year. But most pastors never make it that far. For many, the revival is just around the corner.

Back to the church mentioned earlier. It is Ewart Fork Church of Ewart Fork, Kansas. The pastor is Erik Fleming, and he had no intentions of leaving. He waited on God, and his patience and faithfulness is now bearing fruit.

Welcome to Ewart Fork

The town is indeed small. A few stores, the local school, and a number of residences line the main street.

A recent demographic report clearly shows the more rural lifestyle of Ewart Fork. Nearly 30 percent of the residents within a five-mile radius of the church live in mobile homes. The median value of a single family residence is less than $70,000. Over 30 percent of the residents have a household income under $35,000, while less than 9 percent have incomes over $50,000.

In a demographic survey by lifestyle groups, 86 percent of the population is classified as "blue collar families in small towns." The remaining 14 percent are categorized as "residents of an older, rural town."

I suppose that many pastors, when they dream of their "ideal" church, envision an affluent suburban church with a rapidly growing population. However, if real revival is to take place in our nation, it will happen in the great number of churches that fit a description similar to

132

Ewart Fork's. And it will take pastors committed to invest their lives in such churches. That is why Ewart Fork is on the edge of revival.

Meet Erik Fleming

Erik Fleming has been the pastor of Ewart Fork for five years. In his fifties, Pastor Fleming has had good experiences in other churches prior to coming to Ewart Fork. The pastor has a consistent, calm demeanor. He has experienced the highs and lows of being a pastor, and few circumstances in a traditional church can surprise him.

The pastor's leadership style is one that seeks input and involvement. He does not abdicate his own leadership responsibility. He is the catalyst for change when necessary; but he knows that in a rural traditional church, change must come methodically. The members of the church must own the change before they accept it.

Erik Fleming came to Ewart Fork believing that God was about to do something special. He never stopped believing that promise, even in the more difficult times. He believes that prayer was the impetus behind the growth that the church has experienced. About three years into his ministry at the church, prayer chains formed. Three years later prayer groups were forming spontaneously. One group of men began meeting six days a week at 5:30 A.M., and again on Sunday at 6:00 A.M.

This surge of prayer power was followed by an evening prayer group that began meeting at 6:30 P.M. five days a week. Even the youth joined the prayer efforts, meeting at 11:00 P.M. every Saturday evening.

When Erik Fleming saw what God was doing, he knew that he would soon see the fruits of the prayer, the revival that God had promised. This pastor waited on God, and the wait has been blessed multifold.

Looking at the Growth of Ewart Fork

The statistics that follow will not show a church that has grown exponentially in the past few years. What they do demonstrate is that Ewart Fork has broken an invisible barrier that had not been broken previously.

YEAR	1	2	3	4	5
Average Sunday School Atten.	227	204	190	187	189
Total Receipts ($000)	141	143	139	175	170

	6	7	8	9	10
Average Sunday School Atten.	225	232	243	231	233
Total Receipts ($000)	217	193	191	213	201

	11	12	13	14
Average Sunday School Atten.	227	233	249	256
Total Receipts ($000)	255	215	243	261

Church growth enthusiasts often refer to the barrier that Ewart Fork has experienced as "the 200 barrier." That number reflects the membership of real attenders, those who come at least monthly. It is often reflected as an attendance in the 150- to 250- range. The church will seem to be on a track for growth, but then it will stop or decline slightly.

Ewart Fork, in the first seven years of Pastor Fleming's ministry, had an attendance of 225 to 243, a range of only nineteen. Then the monthly attendance continued to climb gradually. The pattern continues to be healthy to this day.

"The 200 barrier" is typically the result of a single-staff ministry with little or no lay support for ministry. As a consequence the pastor finds that he can only provide ministry to a group that rarely exceeds 200. The church is unable to grow beyond those to whom the pastor ministers.

The most common prescription for a church at the 200 barrier is the addition of staff, or the equipping of laypersons to do ministry. The addition of staff is the simplest but least effective of the two solutions to the problem. The ministry base can expand, but ministry is still limited to the staff.

The biblical solution, according to Ephesians 4:11-12, is for the pastor and other staff to equip and prepare the people of the church to do the work of ministry. While such a solution may seem simple on paper, the process of implementing it can be extremely difficult. Traditional churches can get in the "rut" of a system where the pastor is expected to do all the ministry. If that system is challenged, the resistance can be great. The pastor as the "hired hand" of ministry is one rut that is common.

How does a church overcome this obstacle? Eventually the answer to that question must have a spiritual base rather than a methodological base. Attitudes must change, and attitudes do not change unless God's Spirit is allowed to move freely among His people.

I am convinced that the return of the growth of Ewart Fork is primarily the result of attitudes changed by prayer. For the most part, there is an openness to change and innovation that is not usually present in rural, traditional churches. Sure, the change has to come slowly and methodologically, but it is happening at Ewart Fork.

Explaining the Growth at Ewart Fork

It is my prayer that you who are reading the story of Ewart Fork will be greatly encouraged. The story of the church to this point is not one of rapid growth, but a new spirit that has caused old barriers to be broken. Phenomenal growth may not be God's plan for your church but, through your leadership, God can do great works in your place of ministry. Let us look at some of the factors that have precipitated the growth of Ewart Fork.

Prayer Power

The power of prayer at Ewart Fork cannot be overstated. As mentioned earlier in this chapter, one to two prayer groups from the church meet every day. The emphasis on prayer began with prayer chains in 1988, but the real breakthrough in the church took place when sacrificial prayer began. By sacrificial prayer, I mean prayer that is, at the very least, inconvenient. Can you imagine, in an American church, men gathering for prayer six days a week at 5:30 A.M. and again on Sunday at 6:00 A.M.? It is happening at Ewart Fork. Can you imagine youth having such a burden for prayer that they gather at 11:00 P.M. on Saturday evenings? It is happening at Ewart Fork.

Randy Sanford is the Sunday School director at Ewart Fork. He has been a Christian for only six years. I asked Randy to share with me those events that led to his conversion. "It began with prayer," Randy said. "I grew up in church and became a member when I was about seven years old. After graduating from high school, I quit attending

135

church except for a couple of weeks out of the year. I married my wife, Pat, a few years later, and she began praying for my salvation."

But the prayer efforts did not end there. Randy continues, "Soon a group of people in the church began praying for me. Finally, when I was thirty years old, I gave my life to Christ. I believe beyond doubt that prayer led to my salvation."

Pastoral Commitment

Sit and enjoy the fellowship of Erik Fleming. Drink a cup of coffee with him. Before long you will hear him talk about Ewart Fork Church. You will soon hear him talking about future plans, including his desire to retire in the community. After just a few minutes you will know that Pastor Fleming is committed to stay at the church and in the community.

Most traditional churches are not as fortunate as Ewart Fork. Their pastors come and go every few years. In some of these churches the problem is with the pastors. Some of these men have no intention of seeing their churches through long-term change. The church is only a stepping stone to a "greater" ministry.

Yet in some of the churches, the problem can be found in the attitude of a few people. This group is called many things, but I simply call it the "power group." The group's primary purpose at the church is to retain control. Long-term pastorates threaten their power base, so they find convenient excuses to run off the pastors every two to four years. You often can hear groups of pastors refer to these churches as "pastor-killers."

Ewart Fork is blessed because neither the church nor their pastor desires to end their relationship with each other. The greatest days for the church may be just ahead, because both parties are committed to one another.

Further evidence of Pastor Fleming's commitment to the church is his diligent effort to prepare Ewart Fork for the future. It was he who first contacted me about consulting with his church. He knew that God was bringing the church closer to revival. He wanted to be prepared for God's work rather than be caught off guard. Pastor Fleming had questions about the buildings, the organizations, and the ministries of the church. He wanted to be absolutely certain that he was doing everything he could to be in cooperation with God and His blessings.

Pastoral Leadership Skills

It is a fascinating venture to observe Pastor Fleming's leadership skills. In one particular church meeting I attended, I watched him respond to some questions that implied a resistance to change. Instead of becoming defensive, he handled each question with diplomacy and graciousness, referring some concerns to committees.

Such a process slows the pace of change, but it makes it more palatable to people who value long-standing traditions. The only timetable that concerns Erik Fleming is God's timetable. He has such confidence that God is at work at Ewart Fork that he can be patient and not worry about the future of the church.

That is not to say that Pastor Fleming does not lead the people toward particular goals. To the contrary, the pastor is single-minded when he believes God has given the church a clear mandate. His godly patience combined with his steadfast determination have led the people of Ewart Fork to follow their pastor in new and challenging directions.

Openness to Change

Ewart Fork is a church steeped in traditions in a community steeped in traditions in a county steeped in traditions. One would expect the church to be highly resistant to change. To the credit of its people, however, the church has received slowly some new insights and approaches. Certainly the leadership style of Pastor Fleming has been one factor in their receptive attitude, but most of the people themselves have a hunger for the freshness of God. They are willing to follow because they long to be closer to the God they serve.

Because of the nature of the people and the community, it is difficult to project rapid change at the church. It is heartening to see a church that epitomizes the traditional be willing to change even at a methodical pace. The visible progress may seem slow, but God is at work among the people of Ewart Fork. The change will be soon evident.

Revival Meetings

The success of revival meetings at Ewart Fork cannot be overlooked. In a day when most observers are predicting the demise of traditional revival meetings, here is one church that continues to have tremendous success. Randy Sanford, the church's lay Sunday School director, comments, "I was saved at a revival at Ewart Fork in 1987 at the age of thirty. It is hard to imagine our church without a big revival each year."

How do you explain the exceptional success of Ewart Fork's revivals? The answer is apparently twofold. First the church and the community have a traditional history which still includes revival meetings. Recognizing that traditions can be used for good, the church has utilized this method of reaching people each year. In Ewart Fork, Kansas, revivals are welcomed by the community. The pastor and the people have demonstrated wisdom in retaining an outreach methodology that fits the community's culture, despite the words written by pundits who would have all but abandoned revivals.

A second explanation behind the revival success is the amount of prayer power that precedes these meetings. The people of Ewart Fork believe that God's Spirit will move mightily at each revival, and they pray fervently to that end.

The Challenges that Lie Ahead

Four specific challenges lie ahead for Ewart Fork Church in the next few months and years. The church has broken the 200 barrier. The meeting of these challenges may be the key toward continued growth.

Acceptance of Change

On the one hand, the people have done an admirable job of accepting change in the church. For example, the move to two Sunday morning worship services was accomplished with minimal objections. Only a few members expressed concerns about breaking up fellowship patterns. Multiple services positioned the church to break the 200 barrier as much as any one methodology.

On the other hand, change comes slowly at Ewart Fork Church. The people need to be willing to move faster if more opportunities to reach people for Christ present themselves. I sense that God will challenge the people with some new opportunities in the near future. The response of the people at this point in the church's history will be critical.

Acceptance of New People

Though the population of "greater" Ewart Fork is not exploding, it is increasing. Demographic trends show that new families, particularly younger families, are gradually moving into the community. How the community in general and the church in particular accept the newcomers will be a critical factor in the church's future growth.

Within the next four years the church will probably face a major power shift. It is likely that within this time, the number of active new members will exceed the number of active established members. Will the longer-term members accept this change as positive or negative?

Building Considerations

The members of Ewart Fork recognize the need for more adequate facilities. The initial impression of first-time visitors to the church may be that the church has a lackadaisical attitude about their buildings. These guests may wonder if such attitude exists in other areas.

In my consultation with the church, I recommended that the church renovate their facilities in this priority: preschool space; children's space; restrooms; old education wing; sanctuary; remaining education and office space. This recommendation was contrary to the church's initial thoughts of building a new sanctuary. The relatively large amount of funds needed to build a new worship center could be used to totally renovate the church facilities. And since the church has instituted two Sunday morning worship services, the space is more than adequate there.

The challenge is that the church remain unified in its purpose to get the buildings in satisfactory condition. In a recent meeting, several members expressed various ideas about building needs. While this democratic exchange of ideas is healthy, the church ultimately must move in a singular direction. Those who do not get exactly what they would like for the church are challenged to support the majority of the members and the leadership.

Keeping Prayer as the Focus

Ewart Fork must remember that it broke old barriers when prayer became the priority of the church. The last several months have introduced proposals for the physical facilities and for new methodologies. *The greatest danger for the church at the present is to see these new projects as the solutions to their needs. These projects and methodologies are but tools. Prayer brought Ewart Fork this far. Only prayer will continue the renewal.*

The Church on the Vision Cycle

More than any of the three churches discussed in this section, Ewart Fork has moved along the vision cycle slowly and methodically. The prayer emphases were, in many ways, the key to an outward focus. A very traditional church was able to look beyond itself because its people had a heart for God and His people.

Methodically again, more people have become involved in ministries, particularly prayer ministries. Even some of the youth in the church have increased their ministry involvement significantly. Some began meeting on Saturday night for prayer; large numbers became involved in the youth music ministry.

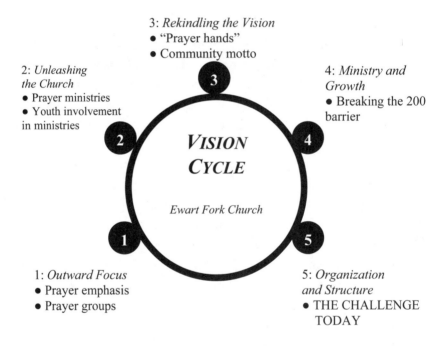

3: *Rekindling the Vision*
- "Prayer hands"
- Community motto

2: *Unleashing the Church*
- Prayer ministries
- Youth involvement in ministries

4: *Ministry and Growth*
- Breaking the 200 barrier

VISION CYCLE

Ewart Fork Church

1: *Outward Focus*
- Prayer emphasis
- Prayer groups

5: *Organization and Structure*
- THE CHALLENGE TODAY

As the outward focus continued and more people got involved in ministry, Pastor Fleming saw that his prayers were being answered. A traditional church could reach its community for Christ. The vision was articulated. Folded prayer hands became the identifiable logo for Ewart Fork. And a long motto expressed their outward focus to the community: "The friendly growing church in the heart of the community with the community in our hearts." The church's vision became clear: the entire community of Ewart Fork would be the mission field.

Steady numerical growth and a deeper walk with Christ became more apparent to the leadership. Lives were changing and the church was growing at new levels. The growth was not astronomical, but it was no less miraculous.

The church finds itself now in need of renewed organizations and structures to accommodate a growing body. Such restructuring would have been impossible or, at the very least, divisive, just a few years ago. Now the church is ready. Thus the efforts have been expended for renovated buildings, new Sunday School classes, and new member assimilation. This point in the life of the church is critical. All indicators point to a successful completion of the vision cycle. Pastor Fleming and the leaders of the church understand the vital importance of new structures. They are steadily leading the church in that direction.

A Church with a Bright Future

The story of Ewart Fork Church is a story of prayer, patience, and persistence. Pastor Erik Fleming has led his church to new levels of spiritual and numerical growth. He has demonstrated the wisdom of waiting on God, while tenaciously pursuing growth and ministry. In fact when asked what the greatest reward of his ministry has been, he responded, "Seeing Christians grow steadily in their faith and their walk with Christ."

Prayer preceded the growth and ministry that is taking place today. Continued prayer is imperative.

Ewart Fork Church will not be included on the "fifty largest churches" list or the "twenty fastest-growing churches in America." In all likelihood it will never become a megachurch or a model church that has conferences year-round. But this traditional church is making a difference for the kingdom. People are being reached and lives are being changed. If one-half of the traditional churches in America would experience the modest but significant growth of Ewart Fork, a revival would sweep our land.

The church does have challenges to meet. But as long as the people realize that the power of prayer is the primary reason for their blessings, both past and future, the days ahead will be days of continued miracles.

Ewart Fork Church—traditional church in a small community. A church with a recent exciting past. A church making a difference. If the people of the church keep their outward focus, remain unified, and stay on their knees in prayer, the best days are yet to come!

CHAPTER 9

TEN LESSONS
FROM THREE CHURCHES

"Wisdom, like an inheritance,
is a good thing
and benefits those who see the sun."
Ecclesiastes 7:11

I am usually the one who receives the blessings. Quite frequently it is my responsibility to speak in a church, to consult with church leaders, or simply to provide the church with some measure of my so-called expertise. But I am usually the one who gains and benefits. I think I learn more than the information I communicate.

For example, my introduction to Calvary Community Church came when I was to lead a revival in the church. My photograph and presumed accomplishments appeared in the local newspaper and other advertisements. I came to give, but I received.

Rarely have I been in a place where the power of prayer was so overwhelming, where miraculous changes were taking place in people's lives—before I ever preached a word! I honestly believe that I could have read the Genesis genealogies and the Leviticus laws each night, and dozens of decisions would have been made. God reminded me once again that church is not first a methodology, but a dependence on the infinite power of a sovereign God.

As an observer of the miracles taking place in these churches, I have been able to gather ten lessons from these traditional churches. Read carefully the next several pages. The lessons that follow may be the most important part of this book. In many ways, the rest of the book is simply an expansion of these lessons.

Lesson One: The Priority of Prayer

I hope our redundancy about prayer sinks in the minds of all of you readers. While good methodologies abound, if everything you do in your church is not bathed in prayer, your efforts will prove fruitless.

C. Peter Wagner wrote a masterpiece on church growth in 1993, *Churches that Pray.* He pleads with churches to give more than lip service to prayer: "Too often prayer is looked upon as a by-product of doing church. It is something that is supposed to happen automatically. It is free. It requires no special effort nor line in the budget. Obviously that kind of an attitude is a sure formula for a church where most talk about prayer is rhetoric and where the results of prayer are virtually nil."[1]

In fact, says Wagner, the key to church growth may be churches that pray and become a part of a revival which is already beginning. "In these days of the great prayer movement sweeping across our nation and around the world, the emergence of exciting possibilities for new and vital prayer ministries in the church is limitless. Churches that hope to have an ear to hear what the Spirit is saying must have a prayer leader who is both called and committed to hearing these things and who is motivating others to full participation."[2]

Calvary, Buck Run, Ewart Fork. All three churches have a commitment to prayer that extends beyond simple prayer chains and Wednesday night "who's who in the hospital." The very lifeline of the churches is prayer. Prayer precipitated the revival in their churches and prayer continues that revival.

A word to pastors who are reading this book: The success of a dynamic prayer ministry in your church will, at least in part, depend upon your own visible commitment to prayer. Do you pray daily for a significant amount of time? Is prayer a focus in your teaching and preaching? Do you lead your people to new depths and ministries of prayer?

All three pastors are prayer warriors. They not only believe in the power of prayer, they practice the power of prayer. Many examples of how pastors emphasize prayer in their churches could be cited. I will give you one such example.

One pastor of a large church in the metropolis of Dallas knows the power of prayer. Because the church is so large, the pastor cannot possibly minister to each member one-on-one. But, on a regular basis, he takes a four-day prayer retreat alone. He informs his church prior to his leaving.

Each church member receives a letter with a return envelope marked "Confidential" and a sheet of paper headed: "Pastor, please pray for this need." The pastor writes to each member, "The letter you write will not be opened until I am alone with God. I will open your letter personally, and pray over your request personally. After I have prayed, your letter will be destroyed. Only three persons will know what you have written: Yourself, myself, and God." Much of the church's vitality and growth is attributed to the leadership of a pastor who is committed to prayer.[3]

Of the churches with which I have consulted, I must say with fear and trembling that many of them do not give priority to prayer. They look to me for the latest quick-fix methodology. Almost every time I write my concluding report to the pastor, I emphasize that prayer must be the true "methodology."

At the conclusion of my consultation at Ewart Fork, I wrote these words to Erik Fleming. My letter concluded by saying, "Erik, all of my suggestions are methodologies and should not be considered an end in themselves. Your church has its focus on Christ and the power of prayer. Do not provide leadership that looks at methodologies as the answer to needs. Keep their focus on Jesus. These suggestions are but a small part of a much bigger picture of Christ's work at Ewart Fork."[4]

Lesson Two: The Security of God's Call

Each of the pastors of the three churches feels certain that God has him where He wants him. They have no sense that they should be in another ministry situation. Bigger churches and higher salaries are not their reasons for their call. They know that no greater peace is available than being in God's will. They are not discouraged by the "success" or size of other churches. Because of their certainty of God's call to their churches, they can rejoice with God's blessings in other places.

Not only are the pastors secure in their call to their particular churches, they are absolutely certain about God's call of their lives to

145

pastoral ministry. Of the three pastors, I have known John Morella the longest. I have seen his life miraculously changed by the power of Christ. I have witnessed God's certain call of him to be a pastor. Never was there any doubt in John's life that God was speaking clearly to him.

I know of one pastor of a large church who has seen many young men in his church called to the pastoral ministry. When one of these men comes to him to share with him his sense of call, the pastor inevitably responds, "Come see me again in one year if you are really serious about this." The pastor believes that if God is really speaking to the young man, then that man can wait a year and the certainty of the call will only increase.

One wise pastor told his son who was sensing God's call, "Try to do anything else. If you find no joy or peace then you will know that God has spoken." The son is now an outstanding pastor, certain of his call.

Now I do not mean to sound judgmental, nor do I claim to know the hearts of pastors. But I have sensed in some pastors a real doubt about their place in ministry. For these pastors, they wonder in the difficult times if they are really in the right place. And a few have confided in me that they know they were not called to ministry.

Pastoring a church, traditional or otherwise, is no easy task. The power of God must ever be present in the pastor's ministry. That pastor must know beyond doubt that his vocation and calling is in the perfect will of God. Pastors Morella, Jackson, and Fleming are certain. That, at least in part, explains the wonderful blessings of God on their churches.

Lesson Three: A Commitment To Stay

Perhaps this point has been discussed more than sufficiently. Yet I will repeat it because of its importance. Each of the three pastors has a commitment to stay at his church. If and when they do leave, I feel certain it will be because of God's call, and for no other reason.

Two of the three pastors, Bob Jackson and Erik Fleming, are in their fifties, so it is easily conceivable that they could retire in their present churches. But even John Morella, who is about twenty years their junior, has no less desire to stay.

Longevity at a church will not, by itself, engender growth. However, it is very difficult for lasting growth to take place when the church has

146

a series of short-term pastorates. The commitment to stay at a traditional church is a vital component of eating the elephant.

Lesson Four: A Desire for Growth

I have met godly pastors in traditional churches who seem to have little or no desire to lead their churches to growth. For many different reasons, they are content with the status quo. Some of them have battle scars and have no desire to again make the effort necessary for long-term growth. Others have fears that growth will bring unacceptable and undesirable changes. A few are just plain lazy and will not put forth the effort to lead a church to growth.

The three pastors cited in this section of the book are hungry for growth and obedient to the Great Commission. They are not "nickels and noses" men to the point that statistical growth is necessary for their happiness. Neither are they content with the status quo and the knowledge that lost people are still in their communities.

While such a statement may seem to be an oversimplification, I believe that God blesses churches where their leaders believe in growth and are willing to pay the price for growth. Several years ago, C. Peter Wagner reported on a nationwide survey of five thousand pastors of various denominations. Less than one-half of these pastors gave a high priority to leading their churches to growth. Said Wagner, "Rather than growth, their priorities were centered on maintenance. Many pastors feel that making the existing church members more comfortable is of higher importance than reaching the lost for Jesus Christ."[5]

Wagner cites five special prices to be paid by the pastor who desires church growth.[6] As I read again the costs of growth to the pastor, I became aware that each of these costs has been paid by the three pastors.

The *first cost* is that the pastor must assume responsibility for growth. Other persons or groups cannot be responsible. When a pastor takes the responsibility for growth, he assumes the risk of failure. Such a price is too high for some pastors.

The *second cost* paid by pastors of growing churches is hard work. Laziness has no place in the lives of the three men who have seen their churches grow. In fact, pastors Morella, Jackson, and Fleming took declining churches and saw God turn things around. While it was

147

God's power at work, they were colaborers in the task. And the task involved a lot of hard work.

A *third price* that pastors must pay is a willingness to share their ministries. A church will not grow if a pastor tries to do everything himself. He must be willing for laypersons and other staff members to assume many of the leadership roles in ministry. That means recognition for a job well done may be gained by someone other than the pastor. And that means that the pastor's ego must be submitted to God.

Fourth, a church growth pastor has to accept that he cannot personally pastor every member. Not only is such a philosophy of ministry incompatible with growth, it is unbiblical. Pastors must understand that one of their primary roles is equipping, in order that other "shepherds" may be trained.

Finally, pastors must understand that a desire for church growth is biblically and theologically sound. Some of the final words of Christ concerned the growth of the church, both in the Great Commission (Matt. 28:18-20) and Christ's ascension (Acts 1:8).

Lesson Five: Survive and Learn from Battles

Each of the three pastors has had his share of battles. Rather than consider the struggles and negative aspects of their pasts, the pastors have learned from them and grown in maturity.

Discouragement and impatience are commonplace in the lives of many traditional church pastors. We so much desire to win the world today, that we cannot understand why our members will not follow our leadership. And when they challenge or criticize us, we have a tendency to become discouraged.

While each of the three pastors has had his moments of discouragement, they were each able to see beyond the battles of the day. Each one knew that God was in control and, that ultimately, the victory would be his.

Lesson Six: Learning Balance in Worship Styles

The style of worship, the type of music, the order of the service, the time of the service, and many other worship-service variables have been among the hottest topics in church growth. I was teaching one of my church growth classes where two of my students were music/worship leaders in their churches. One of them is sold on contemporary music and worship style. He is convinced that the traditional format is a relic of the past that should be quickly abandoned.

On the other hand, the other student was committed to the classic hymns of the past, a formality of worship style, and belief that contemporary Christian music was a device of Satan. Needless to say, we had some spirited discussions in that class!

I have been impressed with the manner in which the three pastors have introduced some of the elements of contemporary worship while maintaining many of the traditional components. Conventional wisdom in church growth and worship literature today says a church must be either/or. If you have a church divided over worship style, you should have multiple services, each with its own distinct style.

I am now convinced that a blended style that slowly introduces some of the more contemporary elements may be best for many traditional churches in the long run. Such has certainly been the case, in different degrees, at Calvary, Buck Run, and Ewart Fork. People of all generations are able to worship together in harmony and joy. Worship styles may be in flux in America today, but I know of three churches that are handling the tension well.

Lesson Seven: Christlike Leadership Skills

What comes to your mind when you think of the manner by which Christ led people while He was on earth? Think about that for a moment. As I looked through the four Gospels I found four major themes in Christ's leadership. Not coincidentally, I found those same leadership qualities in John Morella, Bob Jackson, and Erik Fleming. Let us look at them in brief.

Leadership by Strength

No one can doubt the strength of Christ in dealing with other people. He knew His purpose and He communicated that purpose with clarity and vigor. In His most well-known message to us, the Sermon on the Mount, Jesus communicates clearly to His listeners that living His commands would be the way of wisdom:

> Therefore everyone who hears these words of mine and puts them into practice is like a wise man who built his house on the rock. The rain came down, the streams rose, and the winds blew and beat against that house; yet it did not fall, because it had its foundation on the rock. (Matt. 7:24-25)

On some occasions Jesus demonstrated strength through confrontation. He had little patience with those who were attempting to hinder His Father's mission. To the Pharisees He said, "Woe to you, teachers of the law and Pharisees, you hypocrites! You are like whitewashed tombs, which look beautiful on the outside but on the inside are full of dead men's bones and everything unclean" (23:27). To the same group he said later, "You snakes! You brood of vipers! How will you escape being condemned to hell?" (v. 33).

Leadership by Servanthood

Jesus' leadership style, however, did not always manifest itself in confrontations. More often than not, He demonstrated that a true leader is also a true follower or servant. Jesus would use words like "the least among you" (Luke 9:48) or "deny yourself" (v. 43) to describe the attitude of servant leaders.

Strong leadership is the style of the three pastors. But that strong leadership is framed with an attitude of servanthood which is evident to the three churches. That is why the people are so willing to follow them.

Leadership by Focus

No person ever had to accomplish so much in such little time as Jesus Christ. His entire life and ministry was focused upon doing His Father's will. "So Jesus said, 'When you have lifted up the Son of Man, then you will know who I am and that I do nothing on my own but speak just what the Father has taught me'" (John 8:28).

I am impressed with the focused leadership of pastors Morella, Jackson, and Fleming. It is not difficult to become sidetracked when one is responsible for so many different areas of the church. But these three men keep their churches focused on evangelism, worship, ministry, prayer, and discipleship. Occasional "fires" have to be handled but eventually the focus returns to the primary purposes of the church. In the words of Paul's admonition to Timothy, they "fight the good fight of the faith" (1 Tim. 6:12).

Leadership by Wisdom

Ultimately Jesus would prove to be a perfect leader because he did the will of His Father: "My teaching is not my own. It comes from him who sent me" (John 7:16). The three pastors, though imperfect humans, seek God's wisdom to lead their churches. They know that efforts of the self are eventually fruitless. A significant portion of their prayer life is dedicated to seeking God's will in particular situations in their churches. And God has honored their petitions for wisdom, as promised in his Word (Jas. 1:5).

Lesson Eight: The Importance of Sunday School

For several years I have been monitoring and researching trends in Sunday School. Since the Sunday School has been a key growth, ministry, and discipleship arm in my own denomination, its future has been of utmost concern.

A large number of well-qualified men and women believe that the importance of Sunday School is diminishing. They feel that off-campus small groups will be the look of most churches in the near future. I cannot disagree with the forecasts for small groups. All I can say is that to this point, small groups have not caught on in America as many have predicted. Most churchgoing Americans still desire the more institutional dynamics of Sunday School rather than some other form of fellowship or teaching groups.

The successful traditional church leaders with whom I have spoken still see the great importance of Sunday School. They recognize that the role of Sunday School may be changing, but they nevertheless understand that it may still be the most important organization in the church.

Sunday School is the place where relationships can develop, where people can meet Christ, and where they can be discipled. All three of the pastors still believe that the Sunday School organization is a mighty tool used by God.

Lesson Nine: Balanced Use of Time

In chapter 13 we will look at the topic of time management. For now, we will simply mention that ministry and family demands are extremely pressing upon most pastors today. There is simply no way that a pastor of any size church can say "yes" to all the requests (or demands!) of church members and meet the needs of his family.

In God's wisdom, pastors Morella, Jackson, and Fleming have learned to say "no" at times and have continued to give their families a high priority. Time management is not always easy for them. One of the pastors shared with me that it still hurts him when one of his church members accuses him of not visiting enough. But the three men have stood firm. That is at least one of the reasons God has blessed their ministries.

Lesson Ten: Loving Your Church Members

Let us be truthful, pastors. It is not easy to love everyone in our churches. In fact, some of your church members can be downright unlovable!

In the ministries of the three pastors, however, I have seen a consistency in their unconditional love for their church members. One of the pastors shared with me his "total dislike for Gene (not his real name). In fact, I would go out of my way to avoid him. But then God convicted me. He made me pray for Gene by name every day until I loved him unconditionally. And can you guess what happened? My attitude toward Gene changed and, slowly over time, his attitude toward me changed. Today there is no problem between us."

Is it not ironic that the second greatest commandment is to "Love your neighbor as yourself" (Matt. 22:38), yet we church leaders often disobey that commandment with our own church members? Do you remember the words of John in his first letter? "Dear friends, since God so loved us, we also ought to love one another. No one has ever seen God; but if we love each other, God lives in us and his love is made complete in us" (1 John 4:11-12).

Perhaps one of the primary missions of pastors in all churches, but particularly in traditional churches, is to demonstrate Christ's love in our words and deeds. From that love can flow dynamic leadership for evangelism, discipleship, and ministry.

Fighting the Good Fight

These ten principles from three churches are not practiced without problems. Indeed the struggles can sometimes seem intense and unbearable, but our Lord will see you through all of them. And He will show you how to overcome the greatest of obstacles.

In the final section of this book, we will look at the four greatest obstacles for pastors of traditional churches. Read carefully. You might just see yourself in some of the stories.

NOTES

1. C. Peter Wagner, *Churches That Pray* (Ventura, Calif: Regal, 1993), 93.
2. Ibid.
3. Ibid, 88.
4. Personal letter from Thom Rainer to Erik Fleming.
5. C. Peter Wagner, *Leading Your Church to Growth* (Ventura, Calif: Regal, 1984), 44.
6. Ibid, 46-63.

PART III

VISION OBSTACLES

Most every church leader will recognize the four obstacles which comprise this section. The good news is that these obstacles are not insurmountable. Enjoy reading about them. Even more, enjoy reading about ways to overcome the obstacles.

CHAPTER 10

"WE'VE NEVER DONE IT THAT WAY BEFORE!"

"The indispensable first step
in guiding a church through change
is earning the right to lead the people."
                                        --C. Peter Wagner

You have probably heard about this church. Its story has been in print for quite a while. The church was new, assembling together after the departure of their leader. From a human perspective, their future was bleak. No one outside the church expected them to succeed. Probably some of the church members were wavering in their faith as well, but they tenaciously held to their conviction that something great was about to happen. Well, something did happen. Something almost unbelievable.

This church exploded. From a faithful few, three thousand accepted Christ and were baptized *in one day*. And the growth and conversions continued daily. The church, of course, was the first church. The town was Jerusalem. And the story of the explosive growth is detailed in Acts 1-7.

Now you might expect that such a church would not have to deal with some of the same issues as those of the traditional church. Such unparalleled evangelistic growth may seem to have little in common with the many struggling traditional churches today. But all churches, in different degrees, are confronted with the not-always-so-pleasant constant called change.

I suspect that the first church handled the initial change well. After all, the words of Jesus' promise had been fulfilled at Pentecost: "Do not leave Jerusalem, but wait for the gift my Father promised, which you have heard me speak about" (Acts 1:4). The power of the Holy Spirit was upon the church. Thousands were accepting Christ. The people of Jerusalem were in awe of the church. Excitement abounded. Hope was fulfilled. The rag-tag followers of Christ were making an obvious difference in the kingdom. This type of change probably was well received.

But another major change impacted the church later. Jesus had commissioned the church to be witnesses not only in Jerusalem, but "in all Judea and Samaria, and to the ends of the earth" as well (v. 8). The church responded obediently to the first part of the command; the followers were definitely witnesses in Jerusalem. But what happened to the obedience to the other parts of the command—to extend the witness to all of Judea, Samaria, even to the ends of the earth? Is it possible that the church was satisfied with its work? Was there resistance in responding to leave Jerusalem? Did the change associated with leaving their homes just seem too painful?

Whatever their motives for remaining in Jerusalem, the church did not initially fulfill all of Christ's command. God eventually allowed persecution of the church so that the people would scatter (8:4). Men, women, and children left their homes and moved to other locations to escape persecution. The gospel was proclaimed wherever these believers traveled. Is it possible that such fierce persecution was necessary to initiate change in the early church? Was this action necessary to break up the holy huddles in Jerusalem?

While some of the points are speculative, the central theme is the same: churches have been dealing with change since Pentecost. One of the most important factors in the growth of a church is the manner in which its leaders initiate and handle change. It is especially critical in the traditional church.

Resistance to Change

I should have remembered my seventh-grade year in junior high school. Had I thought about my own personal pain, I probably would have been more careful in changing our church's evening worship format. When I was a seventh grader in Bullock County High School in Union Springs, Alabama, a federal judge ruled that our county school system had to achieve better racial balance. Children would be sent to a particular school according to the zone or geographic region in which they lived. Children from a predominantly black neighborhood would be at the same school as a group of children from a predominantly white neighborhood. My initial reaction was despair! I can still remember coming home and going to my back yard to cry. The cause was noble: racial balance. The intentions of the judge were good. But my secure and comfortable little world had been destroyed.

Had I remembered those feelings, I might have been more sympathetic to the feelings of several church members who were crushed when our staff made the decision to change our evening worship. First, we moved the location from the sanctuary to our large fellowship hall for a more informal atmosphere. Second, we changed the music from traditional to contemporary. Third, we preceded the worship service with a snack supper in the same location as the worship service.

Our cause was noble: to offer an alternative service for our younger adults. Our intentions were good. But I failed miserably in anticipating the response of many of our adults in the forty-five to sixty-year-old range.

One dear lady's visit to my office typifies the feelings of some of our middle-age adults. "Thom, I know you mean well in this move, but it's tearing me apart. Sunday evening worship in the sanctuary, the old hymns, and the fellowship of my peers is central to my spiritual growth." Then her final words made me realize the depths of her pain: "I feel like a major part of my life has been taken away."

When we lead traditional churches to change, we must respect and understand the feelings of those who resist change. Yet, at the same time, if the issue at stake is truly one of eternal importance, we must press on. "We've never done it that way before" is often cited as the seven last words of a dying church. A close relative to that statement is "We tried it before, but it didn't work."

Assessment of the receptivity to change is a necessary early step for the pastor who is to be a change agent. The following chart provides guidelines on a church's resistance level to change. Remember, however, that each church is unique. This chart presents relative receptivity or resistance to change, when all other factors are equal.

Change Receptivity/Resistance Factors for Churches

MORE RECEPTIVE	MORE RESISTANT
Newer church	Older church
Rapid growth in membership	Stable or declining membership
Younger pastor	Older pastor
Pastor with strong leadership skills	Pastor with weak leadership skills
Higher trust level of pastor	Lower trust level of pastor
Previous pastor with short tenure	Previous pastor with long tenure
Longer tenure pastor	Shorter tenure pastor
No dominating family or families	Dominating family or families
Younger membership	Older membership
Regular decision making by staff	Regular decision making by committees, boards, or power groups
Less frequent church business meetings	More frequent church business meetings
Larger portion of membership joined in present pastor's tenure	Smaller portion of membership joined in present pastor's tenure

Principles for Change

Lyle Schaller offers his usual candid opinion when he speaks of change: "Anyone seriously interested in planned social change would be well advised to recognize two facts of life. First, despite the claims of many, relatively little is known about change. Second, much of what is known will not work."[1] Despite his pessimistic outlook, Schaller still encourages leaders to influence the future: "This is the assumption that each of us can learn from the experiences of others, that an anticipatory style of leadership is the most effective style for an era when rapid

160

social change is one of the few constants, and that despite his limitations, man can influence the future."[2]

If understanding change is important for all leaders, it is critically important for pastors of traditional churches. I would imagine that most American churches today fit the descriptions of the "more resistant" categories. In other words, change can be very difficult in a traditional church. Understanding some basic tenets about change will help the traditional-church pastor over many potential hurdles.

1. Begin with Prayer (are you suprised?)

A consistent facet of my prayer life is the prayer for wisdom. "If any of you lacks wisdom, he should ask God, who gives generously to all without finding fault, and it will be given to him" (Jas. 1:5). God-given discernment for a change agent is a requisite. Tough decisions must be made. The promise from God's Word is that He will give us the wisdom in all decisions. The value of all the leadership books and courses in the world pales in comparison to the value of this one promise.

A praying pastor is obvious to the church people. He is dependent on God and demonstrates a humility that comes from dependence. His desire for change is not that he will have his way, but that God's will be done. Resistant people can become receptive people through the power of prayer. If mountains can be moved through faith and prayer, then traditional churches can become open to change through prayer.

2. Love the People

The higher the level of trust of the pastor by the people, the more receptive church members will be to change. While several factors influence the level of trust, none is greater than the pastor's love of the people. Such love cannot be contrived; it must be genuine. A commitment must be made by the pastor that he will love the members of his church unconditionally.

It does not take long for that love to be tested. Cantankerous and critical members will try the patience of the most loving of pastors. How he responds to these people will be both a test of love and of credibility. While he may disagree strongly with a member, his response can be couched in prayerful love.

161

3. Choose Your Battles

I recently read an analysis of a politician's rapid decline in support and popularity. His reelection chances were almost nil because of his unwillingness to compromise. He insisted on having his way on virtually every issue.

Pastors of traditional churches must realize that many issues are simply not worth fighting over. One of my mistakes in changing the Sunday evening worship was making it a major issue for me. Our Sunday evening attendance was relatively small and has declined in the midst of growth in most all other areas of our church. That particular time and day is the most unpopular time for a worship service for the young families in the church. And since our church was growing younger, the attendance had not improved significantly. Our senior adults, for the most part, did not attend because they did not like driving after dark. The group that has the strongest ties to this service was the middle-age adults. If I had sought God's wisdom on this matter, I feel certain I would not have tampered with Sunday evening service. It was not a battle worth fighting.

If our church members see in us a flexibility and willingness to compromise on minor issues, they are more likely to support us on major issues. Of course, any issue that threatens doctrinal integrity cannot be compromised, but the great majority of the battles in traditional churches are not theological in nature.

4. Realize Your Own Imperfections

While I am in a confessional mood, I will share with you another of my "top twenty dumb mistakes." At one of our monthly business conferences, the staff presented a proposal to increase the budget for $30,000 in needed equipment. The questions and suggestions continued for almost an hour until I stood up with foot in mouth and said: "Folks, you called me to be the leader of this church. I wish you would end this discussion and trust us to make the right decision."

The problem was that our proposed purchase was not the best price, and many of our astute business executives knew otherwise. We had consulted no one. My credibility factor took a nosedive that evening. Several months passed before many key leaders began to trust me again.

A strong leader seeks the wisdom of others. A change agent realizes that his way may not be the best way. He admits his mistakes or misjudgments. He is willing to compromise on non-essential items. The effective leader is confident but not arrogant. He has a personality that some might describe as transparent. His confidence is based on his strength in God; his transparency is the result of his willingness to admit his imperfections.

5. Affirm Traditions

Everyone is a traditionalist to some degree. I take the same route home almost every day. I look forward to seeing my wife and three sons. I even feed our two dogs at the same time daily! *Tradition* is not bad. *Traditionalism*, the worship of tradition, is a violation of the first of the Ten Commandments.

We can know that we are practicing traditionalism if our traditions interfere with obedience to God. Sometimes traditions must be broken to reach people for Christ or to be more effective in ministry, but many traditions can be affirmed and celebrated. Josh Hunt describes how John Maxwell had affirmed the tradition of the founding pastor of Skyline Wesleyan Church, Orval Butcher: "Rather than positioning himself in opposition to Pastor Butcher's policies, he has characterized himself as fulfilling that lifelong dream that Pastor Butcher wanted for this church."[3] How has the affirmation of tradition benefited John Maxwell? Josh Hunt explains, "That is incredibly smart. Change management will go more smoothly if past, present, and future are seen as a continuum—an ongoing and direct pathway to what God has purposed."[4]

6. Build on Successes

I know a traditional-church pastor who made a decision after several years of ministry to give credit to the members of his church for any and all of the church's successes. He further decided that any blame for the lack of victories would be his own. Church members would not be blamed; their perceived inadequacies would be the result of his inadequate leadership.

The pastor shared with me that this decision was life-transforming for him. A whole new realm of accountability was created because "the buck stopped" with him. The deacon body, naysayers, or apathetic members would not be blamed. Responsibility would be his. He would do everything in God's power to achieve God's victories in the church. The pastor was directly accountable to God for the church's failures and successes.

By accepting full leadership responsibility for the church, the pastor soon discovered effective leadership skills. He learned that often the best timing for change is soon after a victory or series of victories in the church. Change is often accepted after a leader has demonstrated his ability to lead a church successfully.

7. Allow for Open Discussion

A traditional church has been doing many things the same way for several years. Change can take place, but the pace must be slower than that of a nontraditional church. The people need the opportunity to discuss the proposed change in both formal and informal settings. The discussions in the Monday morning coffee shop may be more important than those in a formal church gathering.

Not only is open communication important, it is also essential that no information be withheld. Every church member should feel that he or she has all the information pertinent to the change. An abundance of relevant information engenders a spirit of openness and trust.

8. Demonstrate Wisdom in Timing

Another one of my "top twenty dumb mistakes" occurred shortly after our church had completed a major building program. In nine months we had made the proposal; initiated and completed a fund-raising program; negotiated construction lending with a local bank; had a churchwide groundbreaking service; and finally entered the new building. All within nine months! The staff and church members were joyful but exhausted.

How did I respond? Shortly after the building program, we presented a major new ministry to start satellite churches. My timing was terrible. The first satellite church was approved, but not without a heavy emotional cost to the church.

Unlike a church planting situation where everything is new, the traditional church is not equipped emotionally to handle rapid change. The timing of each change is critical. Our church probably would have fared much better if I had waited a year before initiating another major ministry.

164

9. Keep the Focus

Up to this point, I have been describing several precautions that the traditional pastor should observe in the process of initiating change. It should be understood clearly, however, that these precautions should not be points of distraction. The leader must ever keep the focus on growing the church. While the pace and frequency of change may be slower and more methodical than the pace in a new or nontraditional church, the traditional church must nevertheless make consistent progress in reaching more people for Christ, and becoming more effective in ministry.

10. Allow for a Trial Period

Some changes may be made on a trial basis. (Obviously a building program would be an exception.) Change-resistant members can be comforted by knowing that the intrusion into their comfort zone may not be permanent. At the end of the trial period, one of three decisions can be made: (1) extend the trial period to allow for further evaluation; (2) reverse the change; or (3) make the change permanent. If the latter choice is made, the benefits of the change will have become obvious to most people. Some members, however, will resist and resent the change regardless of its obvious benefit. Perhaps you have heard the story of the 100-year-old man who was interviewed by a local newspaper. The reporter commented that the old man must have seen a lot of change in his century of life. The man responded: "Yup, and I didn't like none of 'em!" Some church members will see changes but "won't like none of 'em." That observation brings us to the next point.

11. Expect Opposition

We received hundreds of registration cards each worship service. The cards served a multitude of purposes. They told us who was present, both members and guests. They provided space for prayer requests and encourage requests for information. They allowed the member or guest the opportunity to communicate an important decision or commitment, such as a desire to receive Christ. Finally, they served as a general communication vehicle, where anyone can make a comment, either positive or negative.

I retained all the cards with comments directed to me in particular or to the church in general. Once I surveyed a small stack of cards in my "criticisms" file. I was amazed that so many of the critical comments had come from just a few individuals. These were the people who had seen some of the changes in the church, but "didn't like none of 'em." Some people will never be pleased!

Criticism and opposition can drain a pastor emotionally and spiritually. After a while, he may be tempted to refrain from initiating any significant change because of the potential criticism the change may engender. Such an attitude will result in lost opportunities for growth and ministry. The pastor must seek God's wisdom to discern the proper balance between the extremes of being like a bulldozer or a pet rock in initiating change.

Receiving criticism is a fact of life for true leaders and especially for pastors who are making genuine efforts to lead traditional churches to growth. Expect some level of opposition with any significant decision; but love your critics, even the unlovable ones. Show respect for them, even though they may treat you disrespectfully. Pray for them. And keep your eyes on Jesus as you stay focused on growing His church.

12. Evaluate Changes

Not every change is good. Not every change will work. Evaluate decisions on a regular and systematic basis. Be willing to admit that a change did not work. But give a new ministry, program, or idea time to work. Do not concede easily if the change is a deep conviction of yours. Keep on keeping on. The God who gave you the vision will see you through the most difficult of times.

NOTES

1. Lyle Schaller, *The Change Agent* (Nashville: Abingdon, 1972), 11.
2. Ibid., 12.
3. Josh Hunt, *Let It Grow!* (Grand Rapids: Baker, 1993), 128.
4. Ibid.

CHAPTER 11

"I LOVE YOU PASTOR, BUT..."

> "Neither let us be slandered from our duty by false accusations against us, nor frightened from it. . . . Let us have faith that right makes might, and in that faith let us to the end dare to do our duty as we understand it."
>
> -- Abraham Lincoln

Oliver Adderholt was a good pastor. Not a perfect pastor, but a good pastor. He had been with Golden Road Church for three years. For the most part the time with the church had been positive. But Oliver lived with the same problem most pastors face—criticism.

Oliver had learned that criticism comes in different and varying forms. Rarely is the attack direct, but all of the criticisms hurt. One form of negativism that particularly bothered him was the type that was poorly hidden by a compliment: "Pastor, you know we love you, but . . . ." That comment reminded him of the lines that he had recently read in a book: "'It was a good sermon, pastor, but a little long,' is not humorous. You can be sure that the pastor heard only 'but a little long' and carried that around for a few days."[1]

Another form of criticism that was common to Oliver was the "important-petty" comments. Pastor Adderholt was amazed at how some church members made such a big deal over small matters. Carolyn Weese comments that she has "long since ceased to be amazed at some of the criticisms parishioners share with me about their pastors or members or staff."[2] She too is amazed at the pettiness of it all: "People have complained to me that the pastor's Bible is worn out and

167

they wish he would buy a new one. Others complain about the clothes he wears, or that he needs a haircut, or that he doesn't turn his microphone off when he sings and he can't carry a tune."[3]

Perhaps the most irksome to Oliver was "People are saying that . . . ." He thought it was particularly cowardly for church members to hide behind the comments of others. *Let them tell me to my face if they have a problem with me,* thought Oliver. But on second thought he really did not want to deal with a truckload of critics.

The critics this time were particularly vociferous. Pastor Adderholt had been actively involved in the selection of a new staff member. Continuity of staff in this particular case was critical. Fortunately, the former staff member had shared confidentially with him about his potential move a few months before he left. Oliver was able to obtain the resumes and recommendations of several candidates by the time the former staff member left.

When a search committee was formed to look for a new staff member, the pastor shared with the committee the names of several good candidates. He also told them of his prior knowledge of the former staff member's departure, which gave him an opportunity to look for candidates. The committee was very grateful for his work and, as a result, had a candidate to recommend to the church in a few weeks.

That is when the criticisms began. The first came from a particularly negative person who was certain that the selection process was not "by the books." The pastor was flabbergasted by the innuendo. Though the procedure had been swift, he had been faithful to the rules. *In no way,* he thought, *did he deserve that criticism.*

Then came the long, single-spaced, typed letter. The writer had delivered her epistles before, but this one seemed especially harsh and sanctimonious.

The final blow came when Mark, the usual bearer of bad tidings, told Oliver that "people were saying" that the selection process had been "railroaded." *Railroaded!* Oliver shouted to himself. He had done nothing but try to move the church through a possible difficult time. He had anticipated praise from the church for the quick response. No praise ever came. Just criticism and more criticism.

Oliver unloaded his emotions that night with his wife Betty. Together they discussed the events of the past three years. There had been many good times, but the criticisms had been ever present. They wondered together if their brief ministry at Golden Road should end.

Pastors in Pain

Expectations have always been high for pastors. Whether he was an eighteenth-century community pastor for life or a modern-day megachurch pastor, the standards have been high. The Reverend Canon Geoffrey Gray wrote, "People expect their priest to have the skill in sermon preparation of Knox, the oratorical power of Churchill, the personal charm of a film star, the tact of royalty, the hide of a hippo, the administrative ability of Lord Nuffield, the wisdom of Socrates, and the patience of Job. Some people must often be disappointed."[4]

Carolyn Weese says, "Every Sunday morning the pastor is expected to be upbeat, victorious, and enthusiastic to preach a more powerful sermon than the week before. It matters not what kind of week the pastor has had."[5] But there is more. She asks the question, "After all, aren't pastors perfect? They have divine protection from career tensions, family crises, personal struggles, and worry. They don't face the everyday hassles that other people face. What do pastors do all week, besides preach a twenty-minute sermon on Sunday morning?"[6]

Expectations High, Respect Low

While the expectations of the pastor are high, the respect for the position has been declining steadily for years. One of the few consolations a minister has from the ongoing "most respected" polls is that his profession is held higher than that of politicians!

Numerous theories have been proposed about the declining respect for ministers. One position holds that the ministry has become more professionalized, resulting in the same expectations for ministers that one might have for a corporate CEO. Another popular view is the "televangelist theory." Certainly the misconduct of some television ministries can explain the problem at least partially. Finally, there is the view that as our nation has strayed from its Judeo-Christian morality, so has our respect for the clergy who advocate it.

In reality several factors probably combine to account for the

169

declining respect for ministers. Regardless of the explanations, the pastor and other staff ministers are confronted daily with a more hostile environment than years past, and some of the hostility is found within the church.

Carolyn Weese, in her consultation with hundreds of churches around the nation, sees the problem as a common situation: "Congregations fail to realize that pastors have sensitive feelings and that in their capacity as pastors they tend to be more open and, therefore, more vulnerable to criticism than most. *Somehow the people in the pew seem to think they can say anything they like to the pastor and it won't change how he views them or ministers to them.*"[7]

She continues in her amazement at the callousness of some church members: "It is astounding how often well-meaning parishioners—in the name of Christ—will strip down a pastor, expect him to take it, and of course, change his ways instantly to fit their demands."[8] What kind of church member would treat his or her pastor in this manner? She continues, "This kind of treatment is initiated by people who know just enough about the situation to be dangerous and don't care to know the whole story for fear it might save the attack on the pastor. *They tend to resemble vultures feasting on a fresh kill.*"[9]

Tenure and Criticism

One of the continuing themes in this book is that patience is needed for God to do His work in a traditional church. I remain convinced that He desires to breathe new life into stale and staid churches. Yet I am equally convinced that He waits on pastors who are committed to stay with a church. He will send revivals when leaders are in place to guide their churches through those revivals.

When we see God's honor roll in the Bible, we see men committed to their callings and places of service regardless of circumstances. Men like Noah (Heb. 11:7), Abraham (v. 8), Joseph (v. 22), and Moses (v. 24), to name a few, held fast in their callings with patience and courage. And who can doubt the commitment of the apostle Paul? He stayed with God's call despite floggings, beatings, shipwrecks, danger, hunger, thirst, exposure, and imprisonment (2 Cor. 11:23-27).

While most of us pastors would like the tenacity of Moses or Paul, we grow weary from the steady stream of criticisms. Another church, another ministry, perhaps even another vocation becomes very appealing at times. One of my dear pastor friends tells me that his fantasy is to win the grand prize in the *Reader's Digest* sweepstakes! He does not really desire to be wealthy; he simply wants to minister without answering to the critics in the church.

And while I will encourage all of you pastors and staff members to be tenacious in your ministries and churches in the midst of criticisms, I need to speak to laypersons as well. May I be blunt? How do you treat your pastor? Do you offer him words of encouragement? Do you pray for him? Are you willing to overlook minor imperfections?

Or do you hold to the CEO model of leadership? If he does not produce, is he out? Are you so nitpicky about everything he does that he is constantly looking over his shoulder, afraid to move lest he offend someone else?

Most of you laypersons are not divisive by nature. You are supportive of your pastor. But, possibly, when you hear the naysayers speak, you become quiet, lest you disrupt the unity of the church. Wrong! Your silence may be as deadly as the malignant and malicious words that are tossed about in the church. Follow with me in this lengthy quote by Carolyn Weese. Read it slowly. It is critically, perhaps eternally, important.

> Divisiveness is probably the most destructive force found in a church today. The source is usually found in a small core of people. Those people, often without realizing it, work harder at destroying something than at building it up. Because of their enthusiasm for the church and their zeal to make everything "right" in their eyes, they are usually involved in almost every area of the church. It is difficult for the members of the church family to be involved without being tainted by the divisive thrust.

171

Divisiveness spreads through gossip. Truth is embellished with innuendoes, hearsay, and personal conclusions that make the story very convincing. *Divisiveness, in its most effective form, cloaks its actions in the Scripture.* Scripture is manipulated to fit each instance and is preached to receptive people until they cave in.

Divisiveness is so subtle that people do not know they are being sucked into it. Divisiveness is intimidating and controlling. As it becomes stronger, the congregation grows more apathetic and complacent.

Divisiveness is the driving force that splits a church. A divisive spirit can be diminished and eventually eliminated if faced head-on. *The elders or those in leadership positions have the responsibility and authority to rebuke those who would tear down what God is raising up.* They must be strong and of good courage. When they hear gossip, they must shut it down. Strength will weaken and reduce a divisive spirit. [10]

Thus in many traditional churches we have the tension between the need for stability and long-term pastoral tenure, and the criticisms which drain the spirit of the pastor and often prompt him to leave. How can church leaders remain effective in such an environment? Some lessons from the past may help.

A Model for Dealing with Criticisms [11]

Other than Jesus himself, few Christian leaders personify the leadership skills necessary to deal with criticism as Abraham Lincoln did. Though he was not the pastor or staff member of a church, his response to the most malicious critics is a model for Christian leaders to this day.

172

Few people have been slandered, libeled, and hated as much as Lincoln. He was the first Republican president, the result of a divided Democratic party. While Stephen A. Douglas and John C. Breckenridge were splitting votes by region, Lincoln won the election without even being on the ballot in most Southern states.

He was called by every conceivable insult, including baboon, a third-rate country lawyer, a dictator, an ape, and a buffoon. One reporter described him as "The craftiest and most dishonest politician that ever disgraced an office in America."[12]

By the time he became president, Lincoln was the object of intense hatred from many different sides. Though many secular history books fail to mention his decision to respond as Christ would, it was a major reason he was able to lead a badly divided nation. Let us examine the four key aspects of dealing with criticism in the life of Abraham Lincoln.

He Ignored the Attacks

Lincoln's most common response to criticism was simply to ignore it. This response was particularly true during election campaigns where the attacks were petty and ridiculous. Once he became president, he had to focus his energies on winning a war and holding a nation together.

The criticisms hurt Lincoln. Many of them came from people he believed to be his friends. The pain was especially intense early in his political career. He became toughened to the critics later in life, but he never fully adjusted to the barbs thrown at him.

Yet Lincoln knew that he could literally spend an entire career responding to the attacks upon him. He had to decide, with God's wisdom, that most of the criticisms could be ignored. In his last public address on April 11, 1865, he told the audience about his response to the innumerable criticisms: "As a general rule, I abstain from reading the reports of attacks upon myself, wishing not to be provoked by that to which I cannot properly offer an answer."[13]

He Occasionally Responded to Critics

On occasion, however, Lincoln felt it was necessary to respond to some of the attacks. If a vital principle was at stake, if the office of president was maligned, or if the unity of the nation was jeopardized, Lincoln responded. He could overlook petty barbs that hurt him only, but he would not tolerate the compromising of a principle or the unity of the nation.

During one of the Lincoln-Douglas debates, Stephen A. Douglas was applauded enthusiastically while Lincoln was jeered by the crowd. The central issue at stake was slavery. This time Lincoln stood up in public to the critics: "I am not going to be terrified by an excited populace, and hindered from speaking my honest sentiments upon this infernal subject of human slavery."[14]

He Kept His Sense of Humor

Lincoln refused to let his critics take from him his joy for life and his keen sense of humor. His ability to laugh at himself and with others helped him maintain a healthy perspective, while often disarming his critics.

In response to several of Douglas's attacks in 1858, Lincoln told friends: "When a man hears himself somewhat misrepresented, it provokes him—at least, I find it so with myself; but when the misrepresentation becomes very gross and palpable, it is more apt to amuse him."[15]

He Did What Was Right—Regardless!

Abraham Lincoln truly believed that God was with him in his political career. He sought to please his Lord rather than others. As a result, he would enter into the decision-making process with confidence and assurance. Sure, the critics bothered him. He was a mere mortal. But ultimately he kept his focus on that which God led him to do.

Lincoln once said, "It often requires more courage to dare to do right than to fear to do wrong."[16] In a letter to General John McClernand the president wrote, "He who has the right needs not to fear."[17]

When Criticisms Come . . .

Oliver Adderholt is the pastor of a traditional church. He has felt the sting of criticism for doing that which he honestly felt called by God to do. But the attacks have drained him emotionally, physically, and spiritually. He seeks the face of God; he needs the Father's wisdom to deal with the hurt. God leads Oliver to handle criticism in six ways.

The Power of Prayer

Pastor Adderholt rediscovers the abundant power of prayer, especially in dealing with criticism. He claims the promise of James 1:5 for God-given wisdom to handle all situations. He begins to pray specifically for his critics by name. His attitude toward them begins to change. To his surprise, many of the critics begin to change their attitude toward Oliver as well. Prayer opens the pastor's eyes. He learns not to be as defensive as he had been previously. He also learns that he is not always right. The critics are sometimes right, at least partially so.

Furthermore, prayer opens the eyes of Oliver to the real battle. His enemies are not critical church members, but the invisible forces of Satan who have a singular purpose: to thwart God's work (Eph. 6:12). The pastor realizes that when he yields to the distraction of the critics, when he loses his focus upon God's mission, then Satan has won a battle.

The Power of Love

From his prayer time Oliver begins to sense the power of love. By praying for his critics he begins to love them. Those prayers were difficult at first, but he remains obedient to Jesus' mandate to love and pray for our enemies (Matt. 5:44-45). His heart changes as he learns not only to love, but to forgive as well. The pastor realizes that he is a forgiven sinner just like the critics. The grace of God which was bestowed upon him is that same grace available to his enemies.

Learning to Ignore

Abraham Lincoln learned that he could not spend an entire career responding to every criticism. Jesus Himself remained silent in the face of opposition more times than not. Oliver's ego was screaming for rebuttal and vindication in the midst of attacks, but the pastor soon learned that silence was an effective tool. Today's crises and criticisms were quickly forgotten when the issues did not become an open debate.

Learning to Confide

Pastor Adderholt had spent so much time dwelling on the words of a few critics that he failed to realize that the great majority of the church had no idea what was being said. He eventually found a few trusted leaders with whom he could share his frustrations. These men were leaders in the corporate and professional world who had taken their

175

own share of criticisms. They knew how to empathize with Oliver, but they also helped him to keep his focus. "Don't let a few of these buzzards get you off track," Hank Wright responded in his usual blunt manner. Hank was the number two man in the largest bank in town, and he knew well the pettiness of critics. Such comments helped Oliver maintain a balanced perspective and not spend undue amounts of time worrying about detractors.

Respond on Occasion

There will be a few times in Oliver's ministry when a response will be necessary. The issue may be a central doctrinal truth, an ethical concern, or an issue that has the unity and testimony of the church at stake. The problem will be more than just a personal complaint about the pastor.

Because Golden Road Church has seen their pastor handle criticisms with grace, and because they have seen his dependence upon God, they will be inclined to listen when he speaks. They know that Oliver has not blown up at every little problem that has come his way, so his speaking is an indication of the importance of the issue.

The response by the pastor may be painful to both him and the church but, on occasion, it is necessary. He cannot compromise principles and God's Word to avoid conflict. But God is with the pastor. And the Lord will see that good will come from this difficult situation because Oliver truly loves Him and seeks to obey Him (Rom. 8:28).

Keeping Focused

Satan uses divisiveness to keep God's servants out of focus. The enemy knows that the energy which pastors and their church leaders use to combat the critics is energy not available for sharing the gospel and doing God's work.

Oliver Adderholt has learned valuable lessons about criticisms. He never will enjoy them, but he has learned to deal with them. Above all, he is keeping his focus on leading his church toward that which God would have them to do.

By the way, the last time I spoke to Oliver, he was working on a sermon called "Staying Focused." His text was Philippians 3:13-14: "Brothers, I do not consider myself yet to have taken hold of it. But one thing I do: Forgetting what is behind and straining toward what is ahead, I press on toward the goal to win the prize for which God has called me heavenward in Christ Jesus."

Keep pressing on, Oliver!

NOTES

1. Carolyn Weese, *Eagles in Tall Steeples* (Nashville: Oliver Nelson, 1991), 81.
2. Ibid., 81.
3. Ibid., 81 - 82.
4. Ibid., 22.
5. Ibid.
6. Ibid.
7. Ibid., 79, emphasis in original.
8. Ibid.
9. Ibid., emphasis in original.
10. Ibid., 89.
11. The basis for this section is Donald T. Phillips, *Lincoln on Leadership* (New York: Warner, 1992), chapter 6: "Have the Courage to Handle Unjust Criticism."
12. Phillips, 66.
13. Ibid., 69.
14. Ibid.
15. Ibid., 72.
16. Ibid., 73.
17. Ibid.

CHAPTER 12

"IF ONLY WE HAD

MORE MONEY . . ."

"With man this is impossible,
but with God
all things are possible."
Matthew 19:26

The two churches were located in different states, but the similarities between them were amazing. Both churches were in the same denomination. Both churches averaged about two hundred in worship attendance in communities of approximately the same size. The two pastors of the churches were in their early forties and their perspective was positive and visionary. Each church had recently completed a thorough evaluation of itself and its community. The demographics were healthy and the potential for both churches was excellent. On a mild autumn evening in October, each of the churches called a business meeting to present the findings and to make recommendations for immediate action. Let us visit each of these meetings, held seven hundred miles apart.

Newburg Baptist Church began its meeting promptly at 6:30 p.m. A sense of excitement filled the fellowship hall where the meeting was held. The chairman of the task force presented the findings of the group. With minimal remodeling and a new staff member responsible for education and outreach, the church could easily increase its attendance by 50 percent to three hundred in two years.

The study first revealed that immediate increases in attendance could be attained with five additional Sunday School classrooms. The fastest-growing classes were overflowing to the point that no more people could come into the rooms. Attendance increases were impossible because of space restrictions. But the thorough task force found that, with new room assignments and some remodeling, the rooms could be made available. The estimated total cost of the project was $30,000.

The second recommendation addressed the need for a full-time minister of education and outreach. Since the church already had the services of a part-time education minister, the net additional cost of the new full-time staff person would be $15,000.

The response was unbelievable. One of the senior adult class leaders, whose small Sunday School class had met in the same large room for twenty years, spoke first. "Well, I can't speak for all of the ladies in my class, but it seems like we need to be the first to move. Our average attendance is only six or seven, but thirty people could get in the room. Let us be the first to make a move. After all, this is kingdom business!"

One of the "numbers" men in the church responded with equal enthusiasm. "I've done some calculating and figured that we only need to increase our attendance by fifteen to pay for the full-time staff member. I move we amend the budget and take that step of faith!"

Before the meeting concluded that evening, the proposal had been passed with a unanimous vote. The enthusiasm was contagious. The meeting concluded with everyone singing heartily the hymn "Have Faith in God."

However, seven hundred miles away at the Acacia Baptist Church, similar proposals were being made. The responses, however, were vastly different from those at Newburg.

Mrs. Erskine spoke first: "If I'm hearing your recommendations correctly, my Sunday School class will have to move. I don't believe that is fair. We've been in that same room for twenty years. Somebody else needs to move."

Then it was Mr. Flynt's turn: "Do you realize that our personnel costs will increase by 7 percent with this one addition? And once you increase personnel expenses, it's almost impossible to decrease them. I'm firmly opposed to any staff additions."

Initially it sounded as if Mrs. Brown's words would change the direction of the meeting: "Now folks, it seems as if we have the opportunity to reach some people for Christ. We really need to find a way to do so. But . . . we only have $6,000 in the bank. If we only had more money. . . ."

The proponents of the proposal were stunned speechless. Before they knew what hit them, the motion had been tabled for "further study." But the naysayers had their way. The issue would never surface again.

Two years later the attendance of Newburg Church had grown to 326. The attendance of Acacia Church was 163.

Two Churches, Two Responses

How could two churches of such similar circumstances and opportunities respond in opposite fashion? Let us examine characteristics of both churches as they relate to their past and to their future.

The View of the Past

Newburg Church celebrated its past. The thirty-year old church constantly reminded itself that it was the fruition of the dreams and faith of a small number of visionaries. The past served as a reminder to move forward, to seek new and challenging ways to reach people for Christ. The past was the promise that God works miracles if His people are open to His will. They would never get comfortable, but would always be willing to take steps of faith.

Acacia Church remembered its thirty-four-year-old past as well. Many of the people remembered the birth of the church and the construction of the new buildings. And a great number of the members longed to hold on to "the way we've always done things." Change was frightening to Acacia because it meant to them a departure from the "good old days" of earlier years. Almost anything new was viewed as evil because it was different from their church of the past.

The View of the Future

The people of Newburg Church are excited about the future. The days ahead present opportunities for ministry and growth. They have the faith that God will supply all their needs to reach their community. In essence the future will be better than the past or the present, because God's greatest blessings are yet to come.

181

The future frightens the naysayers at Acacia Church. They are worried about building costs and personnel costs, and they are worried about change. Their worry goes beyond prudence or fiscal responsibility; they simply do not trust God to provide. The future is further a threat because it represents the potential to be different from the past. The past is security and comfort; the future is insecurity and discomfort.

The best times for the people of Newburg Church are viewed to be in the days yet to come. The best times for the people of Acacia Church have already taken place. Both churches will be proven correct in their perceptions.

The View of the Church Size

Newburg Church, primarily because it has a future mindset, sees itself as a large church. When the church was averaging two hundred, they realized that they were larger than 75 percent of all churches in America. And when their attendance surpassed three hundred they really felt like a large church.

The people of Newburg made plans with a larger-church mindset. They planned for future staff, more space, and larger budgets. They dreamed of new ministries and new outreach possibilities. They never thought they were too small to do God's will in their community.

Acacia Church, on the other hand, saw itself as a small church with limited potential. As a result, most of the decisions made by the people of the church were to protect the status quo and to avoid further losses. They tenaciously held on to their church ideal: their church of the late 1950s. Because of its perceived smallness, the church struggles for growth. The people become cliquish because new members are a threat to fellowship groups and the status quo.

A visionary pastor will often become frustrated at churches like Acacia. If he seeks new members, the older members may feel threatened and neglected. Content with the status quo, they resist any new suggestions or proposals. Further, they may be controlling and possessive of the pastor and all that he does. Carolyn Weese notes that "they feel that if they are putting something in the offering plate, they have permission to tell the pastor when and how to do ministry."[1] And many times the pastor decides not to resist their control: "The pastor becomes owned by the congregation to the extent that he may feel little freedom to build ministries according to God's leading; instead, he capitulates to the wishes of the congregation."[2]

The "We Can't" Obstacle

Acacia Church is the epitome of the "we can't" obstacle. It is almost unbelievable to visit and consult with hundreds of churches that act as if the God they serve is taking a nap for a few hundred years. The "we can't" attitude manifests itself in several areas. Let me highlight a few.

Not Enough Money

Perhaps the most common stumbling block is the perception that the church just does not have the financial resources to do what they should be doing. Let me share a secret with church leaders, both lay leaders and staff. I have been in churches of all sizes, in every conceivable demographic situation, with every possible growth rate. And guess what? All of the churches believe they need more money and larger budgets. Everyone of them dreams of the possibilities in their church with greater financial resources.

The difference between "can-do" and "can't-do" churches is how they respond to their present financial situation. "Can't-do" churches will literally stop doing many ministries because they do not have the money. They certainly would not consider any new ventures.

The "can-do" churches, on the other hand, will often go into new ministries without a clear indication of the financial resources available for the venture. They do not act irresponsibly; they act on faith.

The attitude of the "can-do" church is that God does and will provide everything they need to do His will. They do not compare themselves with other churches and, in pity, bemoan their lack of resources. "Can-do" churches simply trust God for their finances. And God honors their faith.

The Problem with the Building

I have earlier spoken of attitudes about church buildings. "Can't-do" churches like Acacia see limitations on growth because of the building. Not enough space. Not enough classrooms. Cannot afford to add to or change the structure. Because of such an attitude, the building becomes the limitation to the growth and future of the church.

The difference between Newburg and Acacia was one of attitude. Newburg was able to raise a relatively small amount of funds to accomplish some needed renovations for space. Acacia could not see the possibility of raising funds, nor would they make the changes if the money was given to them.

Limitation of Programs and Ministries

Oftentimes when I visit smaller churches which are in close proximity to larger churches, an attitude of defeatism may be present. "We just can't compete with Eagle Run Community Church. They have so many programs and ministries. Why would anyone come to our church when they have so much more to offer?"

Well, I have good news for smaller churches. Over one-half of the people in America prefer a smaller church, less than two hundred in attendance. Instead of bemoaning their lack of programs and ministries, churches across our nation need to celebrate what God has given them.

The nonmegachurches of America should also view themselves as specialists who can do a few things very well. The focus may be on a certain age group or a particular ministry. It probably will not be possible for your church to meet every need and every request. That is okay. That is why God gave us so many churches. Do not cry over what you do not have. Celebrate what God has given you, and reach many for Christ.

Staff Limitations

I recently spoke with the pastor of a church where almost one hundred single adults were in attendance on a given Sunday. While that number is impressive on its own, what is more impressive is that the church has less than three hundred in average attendance. What super staff person has led the church to such outstanding outreach? Actually, there is no staff person of the three full-time ministers who has responsibility for single adults. The ministry is led by a layman who feels called to single adult ministry, but also feels called to keep his job in the corporate world.

Once churches of all sizes get out of the mindset that a vocational minister has to initiate and maintain a ministry, then the supposed shortage of staff will not seem so critical. In fact, laypersons usually offer continuity and stability to ministries that the mobile ministers cannot always offer.

184

Yet there will be times that staff additions will be necessary. The church will be faced with the choice of being a "can-do" Newburg Church or a "can't-do" Acacia Church. The church must maintain the balance of being financially prudent while taking the steps of faith to which God has called them.

Overcoming the "We-Can't" Obstacle

Thousands of traditional churches in every part of our nation are powerless and largely ineffective. Many of the people in these churches see earthly obstacles—lack of money, building limitations, inadequate staff, etc.—but they cannot see the power of God which is sufficient to overcome any obstacles. How can pastors lead their churches toward a mindset that believes in God's possibilities? Let us examine five possible strategies.

Prayer . . . Again!

My constant mention of prayer throughout this book is not coincidental. Many of our traditional churches are in dire straits. A miracle is needed for a new attitude and an openness to God's work. It can happen! Ask God. I love the New International Version translation of this verse: "The prayer of a righteous man is powerful and effective" (Jas. 5:16).

Do you believe attitudes can be changed with prayer? Do you believe that your prayers for your church can be powerful and effective? Take God at His Word. There is no such thing as a helpless and hopeless church. God may be waiting on your prayers for miracles to take place.

Develop Allies

Shortly before writing this chapter, my wife and I had dinner with another pastor and his wife. My pastor friend told me of one particular man in his church who attempts to bring a negative slant to every business meeting. When the man stands to speak, others look at him with dagger-like eyes, but he still dominates the meeting and sets a negative tone for the evening.

Pastors and other church leaders need allies who can pray with them, talk with them and see God's possibilities for the church. Quite often the positive church members are intimidated by the actions of a few recalcitrant individuals. As you develop allies, you will have a solid core group that will gain confidence to speak positively in both public and private settings. It may even be advantageous to ask these allies to lead the discussion on important issues. Their words can set a positive tone and possibly silence the ever-present critics.

Focus on the Church's Strengths

Not even the largest churches can meet everyone's needs. God has given you church people with their own unique giftedness. He has also placed your church in your community for specific reasons.

What are the strengths of your church? What aspect of your church's ministry can be celebrated and promoted? Help your people to focus on the ways that God is already working in your church. Take the spotlight off the ministries and programs your church does not have. Make your present and potential ministries be the focus. Seek ways to strengthen those ministries and programs. Celebrate the blessings God has given you.

Challenge the People

A hunger is present in most Christians' lives. A hunger to do something great for God, to be someone different for the kingdom. Church members may act satisfied with the status quo; indeed they themselves may think they are content. But deep inside the heart of every Christian is a desire to break out of the shell of the common and to be a part of something miraculous.

The people of your church, especially those staid traditional churches, need to hear from you about God's power. They need to rediscover the power of the Holy Spirit who dwells within them. They need to hear sermons about Simon Peter, who walked on water when he had his eyes on Jesus, but who sunk into the depths of the sea when he looked to the side at his difficulties and problems (Matt. 14:28-32). The people need to know that the normal Christian life is one of victories and even miracles. As one preacher said, "Christians must forever depart from the sameness, the lameness, and the tameness for life."

But you—pastor or staff member—you need to believe in the power of God yourself. Your life must be one of victories and faith. You cannot lead a people to a promised land unless you have known the miracle of deliverance.

I have been in churches that are at death's door. I have also seen some of those churches become vibrant testimonies in their communities when the pundits said it could not be done.

Challenge your people. Reintroduce them to the God of miracles. Help them to dream again. Lead them to open their eyes to God's possibilities. And remember the words of the Savior: "With man this is impossible, but with God, all things are possible" (Matt. 19:26).

> When things go wrong as they sometime will,
> When the road your trudging seems all uphill,
> When the funds are low and the debts are high,
> And you want to smile, but you have to sigh,
> When care is pressing you down a bit,
> Rest if you must, but don't you quit.
> Life is strange with its twists and turns,
> As everyone of us sometimes learns,
> And many a failure turns about,
> When we might have won had we stuck it out;
> Don't give up though the pace seems slow,
> You may succeed with another blow.
> Success is failure turned inside out,
> The silver tint of the clouds of doubt,
> And you can never tell how close you are,
> It may be near when it seems so far;
> So stick to the fight when you're hardest hit,
> It's when things seem worst
> That you must not quit.
>
> -- Unknown

NOTES

1. Carolyn Weese, *Eagles in Tall Steeples* (Nashville: Oliver Nelson, 1991), 33.
2. Ibid.

CHAPTER 13

"WHY DIDN'T YOU VISIT ME?"

> "Whenever you become overbusy and pressured to do too many things in too short a time, realize that you are not even close to being in demand as Jesus was."
>
> -- Carl F. George and Robert F. Logan

Meet Art. Art is the pastor of the West Cove Congregational Church in Bryan, Texas. Like many pastors, Art does not really have a typical day; but we are going to follow him around on this particular Tuesday. We will see if his day has any unusual twists to it.

West Cove is a typical traditional Texas church. Average worship attendance is 180, and the church has experienced modest growth in Art's tenure of four years. The pastor has experienced highs and lows in his time at West Cove, and there are no major problems in the church of which he is aware.

The alarm awakens our friend rudely at 6:00 a.m. For the next one hour or so, Art helps his wife get three children ready for school. Then he shaves, showers, and heads to the church by 8:15 a.m. He greets his secretary and begins preparation for one of his sermons by 8:30 a.m.

Thirty minutes into his sermon preparation, his secretary calls on the intercom. Betsy Franks has been taken to the hospital with chest pains. Art marks his place in his commentary and takes the twenty-minute drive to the hospital. He stays with Betsy and her family until the danger has passed and heads back to the church. He arrives at 11:30 a.m. and decides to skip lunch. He really needs to study.

At 1:00 p.m. the secretary reminds him of the committee meeting at the local church association. "Can't I get out of it?" he complains. The secretary responds with mild empathy: "No way." Art is the committee chairman.

Finally at 3:00 p.m. he settles back into his office, ready to hit the books again. The intercom again. "Your 3:00 p.m. appointment is here." What appointment? he wonders. His calendar answers his question. The Michaels are in for counseling. Marriage is shaky. Art meets with them until 4:30 p.m.

A small stack of telephone calls awaits the pastor after the counseling session. He decides to do his correspondence for an hour before returning the calls. That will give him thirty minutes to return the calls, thirty minutes for supper with his family, and then on to his 6:30 p.m. appointment at the Wilder's home. They are prospects ready to join the church.

The last telephone call to return is Mrs. Ikerd. Art saved it for last, dreaming that the message might just disappear. He takes a deep breath, dials the number, and waits. "Hello, Gladys, this is the pastor returning your call." The other voice responds: "It's about time! I called four hours ago!"

Art bites his lip and says calmly, "What can I do for you, Gladys?" The church member responds with sanctimonious indignation: "Pastor, people are talking. They don't believe you are spending enough time in the office, and there have been tons of complaints about the fact that you don't visit enough. I bet you didn't even care that I was sick with the flu all last week. Why didn't you visit me? . . ."

The "Arts" of this World

Every pastor can identify with Art regardless of the size of the church. Pastors are in an occupation that is the epitome of paradox. On the one hand, the job has no direct supervision. The pastor's schedule is flexible. He has the freedom to be a total goof-off or a hopeless workaholic. Most pastors lean toward the latter.

On the other hand, a pastor reports to everyone. Each church member is his boss. They pay his salary, so they think they have every right to keep him in line. Several years ago I gave a survey to the deacons of the church where I was pastor. I simply listed several categories of pastoral responsibilities and asked them to share with me a reasonable amount of time spent on each responsibility. The following illustrates the highest hours per week suggested by any one deacon:

Prayer	14 hours
Sermon preparation	18 hours
Outreach visitation	10 hours
Counseling	10 hours
Hospital and home visitation	15 hours
Administration functions	18 hours
Community involvement	5 hours
Denominational involvement	5 hours
Church meetings	5 hours
Worship services/preaching	4 hours
Other (cumulative)	10 hours
	114 hours/week

If I had just met the expectations of all the deacons, I would have had less than eight hours a day available for meals, sleep, family time, and leisure activities. Clearly the pastor will sense the tension of the various factors competing for his time. How he handles that tension may very well determine if he will lead this traditional church to growth.

Time Management and Growth Potential

Several years ago I heard a message by Charles Swindoll where he used the phrase "tyranny of the urgent." He was specifically referring to Christians who spend their lives going from one crisis to another. Organized lives with ample time for prayer, Bible study, and friends is little more than a dream.

Pastors and other church leaders experience the tyranny of the urgent as much as any group of which I am aware. Before I sensed God's call to vocational ministry, I would envy all the time I believed pastors had. They could spend their days in hours of prayer and study of the Bible. Oh, they might have an occasional wedding, funeral, or hospital visit; and they would have to prepare sermons. But, for the most part, the pastor's time was hours of spiritual retreat. Wrong!

A leader in a traditional church will feel considerable tension in time management. On the one hand, traditional church pastors are often expected to be directly involved in time-consuming one-on-one ministry. On the other hand, such ministries dilute the time available for outreach and equipping ministries.

Many church growth books indicate an inverse relationship between pastors who do ministry and the growth potential of the church. I would agree that prospects for church growth are not as good for the pastor who *literally wears himself out* meeting the needs of every church member. Yet I would not carry that principle to the opposite extreme. *A pastor of a traditional church who does little or no personal ministry is setting himself up for major problems in the future.*

Such is the tension that must be managed by the pastor: time spent in equipping ministries for church growth and time spent in personal ministry for trust and credibility. The pastor of the traditional church who decides to devote almost all of his time in equipping ministries will soon hear the complaints: "He doesn't have time for us"; "He cares more about growing a church than ministering to his members"; and "He is not a very warm person."

Traditional church pastors will not solve the problem of this tension. They must learn to deal with it and live with it. Balance and good time management are keys to living with the tension. Let us examine some basic time management tools.

Keep Track of Your Time

Management guru Peter Drucker said, "Everything requires time. It is the one truly universal condition. All work takes place in time and uses up time. Yet most people take for granted this unique, irreplaceable and necessary resource. Nothing else perhaps distinguishes effective executives as much as their tender loving care of time."[1]

Do you know how every minute of your day is spent? Have you ever kept a time log for two or three days? Did you know that you can change your behavior just by recording your time? Are you spending adequate time on those areas which are most important to you and God?

Become a Better Steward of Time

In my years of church consultations, I have seen one particular area that consumes large chunks of a pastor's time: hospital visitation. Pastors in small towns and rural areas often must travel to other cities to visit their hospitalized church members. City and suburban pastors often find themselves going from one section of the city to another.

In this area of ministry and others, church leaders need to plan their day carefully. Except for emergencies or life-or-death situations, a few minutes with each hospitalized church member is adequate. In fact, a sick person usually welcomes a brief visit.

One church consultant listed the most common time wasters for ministers. See if you can identify with any of these: "television, reading the newspaper, running errands others could do, self-imposed interruptions (studying and finding something else interesting on your desk), no to-do list, opening useless mail, overpreparation, handling mail or paper four to five times, driving, unstructured visitation, not having clear directions, spending too long visiting, work overload diminishing output, ineffective reading habits, telephone, not getting up early enough and procrastination."[2] Can you make improvements in any of these areas?

Establish Priorities

If the "tyranny of the urgent" is one problem for ministers, the "captivity by the mundane" is another. How many hours do we spend each week on tasks that are relatively unimportant?

Charles Schwaab, then president of Bethlehem Steel, brought in management consultant Ivy Lee for one primary need: help the president discover how to get more done in the same amount of time. Mr. Lee took a three-by-five card out of his pocket and gave it to Mr. Schwaab. "I want you to write down the things that need to be done tomorrow, in the order of their real importance. When you come to work tomorrow, I want you to work on number one until it is completed. At the end of the day, write a new list. Try this system as long as you like, then have your staff try it. Evaluate this activity, and send me a check for what you think it's worth."

In a few weeks Mr. Schwaab sent Mr. Lee a check for $25,000![3] Such may be the value of establishing your priorities.

Become Organized

Do you find yourself going from one task to another with virtually no system or organization? Learn to group your activities. Set aside one hour or less to return telephone calls. Block out entire half-day segments for sermon preparation.

One time-management expert recommends that we divide our work week into forty-two four-hour segments. We can thus plan each day by six different activities: family time and sleep, church meetings, study time, etc. We do not become as easily frustrated with minute-to-minute interruptions, because we work in four-hour segments.

Simple devices such as palm pilots, calendars, to-do lists, organization files, and a basic planning system can save hours of a church leader's time. Common sense management skills such as handling all your mail at once will give you more time for both outreach and Mrs. Smith's home visit.

It's OK to Say No

Pastor, you will never have enough time for anything until you learn the magic of the little word no. You cannot do everything. You have responsibilities to God for prayer and Bible study. You have responsibility to your family. You have responsibility to your church to preach, shepherd, and equip. You have responsibility to yourself for rest and leisure activities.

Do you realize that, in the long-term, you are actually hurting your church by saying "yes" to all of their requests? The members of your church need to learn (perhaps at an elephant-eating pace) that they do not need you for every meeting, social, activity, or ministry. As you sever the bond of pastoral dependency, and equip your people for doing ministry, your church will become healthier and more productive.

The Power of Delegation

Not only can you say no, you can also empower others to do ministry and activities. One of the most-often stated lines to me by a church member used to be, "Pastor, our church needs . . . ." Early in my ministry I began responding with, "That's great! And I believe that God has given you that burden. You are now chairman of an ad hoc group to make recommendations and to implement this need. Let me know of your results."

Needless to say, the "our church needs . . ." comments became much less frequent. But many still shared with me opportunities for ministry, and they did take charge. I empowered them for ministry and equipped them as best I could. Many new ministries and activities began that were lay-started and lay-led. And my time was protected for other priorities.

Learn to delegate! You may think that no one can do it better than yourself, but you will do nothing well if you try to do it all.

When Spiritual Gifts Are Discovered . . .

I find myself returning to 1 Corinthians 12-14 again and again in my ministry. This passage, and the spiritual gifts passages in Ephesians 4:11-13 and Romans 12:6-8, are critical in our understanding of the proper stewardship of time resources.

C. Peter Wagner has been one of the major forces in the Church Growth Movement. Of all the contributions he has made, one of the major ones has been his discussion of the relationship between church growth and spiritual gifts discovery. Concerning time management and spiritual gifts, Wagner says, "While the church is subject to many principles of human organizational management, it is much more than a mere human organization. It is the Body of Christ. It is an organism with Jesus Christ as the Head and every member functioning with one or more spiritual gifts."[4]

The result of a church functioning according to spiritual gifts is a church where the work of ministry is distributed to every member. No church member, including the pastor, has an excessive burden. Says Wagner, "God does not bring people into the Body of Christ as spectators. He expects them to participate in the life and work of the church just as the various members of our own physical bodies contribute to the well-being of the whole."[5]

Spiritual gifts discovery has two primary benefits in the area of time management. It frees the pastor to do his ministry according to his giftedness and passions. And it empowers the people of the church to be in ministry which might otherwise fall in the overloaded hands of "hired help." Since we looked at the mechanics of spiritual gifts discovery in an earlier chapter, we will focus now on those two benefits.

195

Spiritual Gifts Discovery by the Pastor

As I visit and speak with church leaders across our nation, I am amazed at how few of these leaders know their own spiritual gifts. Meeting the needs of others is next to impossible until we leaders know ourselves.

For example, when I was a pastor, I discovered counseling was one of my weaknesses. Two prominent gifts I have are administration and evangelism. But the rest of my spiritual gift mix is not conducive to a counseling ministry. This awareness led me to take some steps that increased my personal ministerial efficiency greatly.

First, I realized that I would have a tendency to place counseling responsibilities on the back burner since my gifts are not in this area. But, as a pastor, I could not relinquish all counseling responsibilities. So I would make special efforts to make myself available and open to my people. I could not give them the impression that I do not care for them or that I do not want to see them.

Second, I was honest with my church members that counseling is not my strength. I would always have an open door for them but, in the long-term, others could help them more than I can. And that statement brings me to my final step.

Third, I would delegate counseling responsibilities when possible. Two laypersons were trained and equipped to handle a large portion of the counseling load in the church. A staff minister who had spiritual gifts, which were more compatible with a counseling ministry, handled much of this ministry. Finally, I would refer some members to Christian psychologists in our area.

The point is simple. I knew my spiritual gifts. I knew where I was not gifted. So I made plans to strengthen my strengths and compensate for my weaknesses.

Spiritual Gifts Discovery by the Church

Little more needs to be said about the importance of spiritual gifts discovery by the people in the church. From a time management viewpoint, the more people are involved in ministry, the more time a church leader will have to do the tasks God has called him to do.

The Importance of a Leadership Team

In Carl F. George's and Robert E. Logan's book, *Leading & Managing Your Church,* the authors cite the importance of a pastor developing a leadership team to equip and encourage. Time spent in this area could very well be some of the most productive time in the pastor's ministry. George and Logan give five steps in the development of the team.[6]

1. Focus Your Time and Energy to Equip Current Leaders and Develop Future Leaders

Most pastors of traditional churches spend their time and energy on those who complain the most. Such people are a drain emotionally, physically, and spiritually to the pastor. Though the negative people cannot be ignored, the focus of the pastor's time should be on the positive and teachable people.

2. Select and Recruit People with Leadership Potential

If the pastor equips just two or three potential leaders, the benefits will be extraordinary. A potential leader will be obvious to most people. Some of the characteristics to notice are: (1) a love for God and man (Matt. 22:37-40); (2) a willingness to serve (Matt. 20:26); (3) a willingness to learn (Phil. 3:12-13); and (4) growth in Christian character (1 Tim. 3:1-13).

3. Agree on Areas for Training and Development

Aulene Maxwell, the director of the prayer ministry of a church I pastored, was a self-starter. Yet we on the staff spent more time with her than many other members. We were constantly trying to provide her with new information and areas for training. We would talk to her about seminars, speakers, and videos. We agreed that training for prayer ministry leadership will be the focus of our efforts.

4. Recognize the Dynamics of an Effective Training Program

George and Logan point out that the American education model is a three step process: orient, equip, involve, in that sequence. But Jesus trained His disciples in the order of orient, involve, and equip. People learn first by doing better than by receiving factual information. One of the ideas behind the Doctor of Ministry program in seminaries is to provide training after a minister has been on the field. Our formal education makes more sense after we have experiences in the real world. Such is the case for discipling lay leaders.

5. Schedule Regular Appointments for Ongoing Reporting, Encouragement, and Accountability

The final step in building a leadership team is to stay with your leaders. Be mutually accountable to one another. Give them encouragement and affirmation. And watch your own life and ministry grow as new leaders are developed in the life of your church.

"So . . . Why Didn't You Visit Me?"

We met Art, the pastor of West Cove Congregational Church, at the beginning of this chapter. He had encountered the ever-so-common obstacles in a traditional church of time constraints and ministry demands.

Will the time-management principles stated in this chapter solve all of Art's ministry demands? Or yours? No. The tension will always be present. The expectations of a traditional church pastor are high, but you can see your situation improve. You can find more time available for vital ministries.

And lest you forget, the implementation of every principle stated in this chapter will take time. I know I sound redundant by this point, but eating an elephant is a bite-by-bite task that can take years. And leading your church over the time constraint obstacle may take years as well. But it can be done. Wait on the rewards.

NOTES

1. Peter F. Drucker, *The Effective Executive* (New York: Harper & Row, 1985), 26.

2. Carl F. George and Robert E. Logan, *Leading & Managing Your Church* (Old Tappan, N.J.: Fleming H. Revell, 1987), 43.

3. Cited in George and Logan, 45.

4. C. Peter Wagner, *Leading Your Church to Growth* (Ventura, Calif: Regal, 1984), 132.

5. Ibid. For his full monograph on the subject, see C. Peter Wagner, *Your Spiritual Gifts Can Help Your Church Grow* (Ventura, Calif: Regal, 1979).

6. George and Logan, 106 - 12.

PART IV

CONCLUDING THOUGHTS

We now conclude the journey. In this final section we bring together many of the major themes of the book. Thanks for joining us. We pray that God in some manner spoke to you through this writing.

CHAPTER 14

PUTTING IT ALL TOGETHER: THE GROWING TRADITIONAL CHURCH

> "He has showed you, O man,
> what is good.
> And what does the Lord
> require of you?
> To act justly and to love mercy
> and to walk humbly with your God."
>
> Micah 6:8

I have enjoyed this journey with you. You see, I am one of those obnoxious optimists who believes that revival is coming to many churches across our land, particularly traditional churches. I am not alone in my belief.

C. Peter Wagner looks beyond methodologies for the true growth that he believes will happen. Says Wagner, "There is an awesome feel about what is now going on. No one in my generation has experienced true worldwide revival, so we can only imagine what it might feel like."[3] Wagner anticipates that the revival might be soon: "My sense is that most of us alive now will live to see the great revival. I cannot set dates, but it does seem as if this is the generation that will experience the greatest outpouring of the Holy Spirit in perhaps all of history."[4]

Why am I sharing these beliefs about revival? The primary reason is that God already seems to be sending "mercy drops" to traditional churches as a possible forerunner to the "showers of blessings" that will come. It is my unshakable conviction that the sovereign God is waiting to do a mighty work in your church.

You may be weary. You may be discouraged. You may have so many battle wounds that you are just not sure you are up to leading your church one more day. Please hear my words of encouragement: God is not done with you yet! The best days may just be around the corner.

Look at the vision cycle for your church. It is a fallible tool, but I think it gives a perspective on the steps that can be taken in your church. Do you remember them?

1. Outward focus
2. Unleashing the laity
3. Rekindling the vision
4. Growth and ministry
5. Organization and structure

Now, because the vision cycle is no more than a visual tool, you may see one particular area that needs more work. So you "skip" a step. That' s OK! The cycle has been given to help you, not to confine you to yet another set of legalistic rules.

As you move along the cycle, wait with anticipation that God's revival will come. It takes a lot of patience to lead a traditional church, but you can do it. You have the presence and promise of the Spirit. You will experience several tensions but you can handle them.

Tensions of the Traditional Church Pastor

As you lead your church to growth, you will have to demonstrate a great deal of balance. Being a traditional church pastor is an exercise in paradox. Look at a few of the tensions that you must keep in balance.

Spiritual and Pragmatic

You must give priority to prayer. Yet you must be open to new methodologies that could help your church grow. You will need to be a consumer of the latest church growth literature, but you must realize that only a sovereign God can send real revival. You must depend totally on God, but not take lightly the counsel of godly men and women. You must ask "What works?," but you must realize that tools are only for a season.

202

Tenacity and Flexibility

Because you are the pastor of a traditional church, long-term tenure is of great importance. Unless God clearly calls you to another ministry, you will need to be tenacious about your calling, even in the most difficult of times. Satan would love to see you so discouraged that you are ready to give up.

Yet while you must be unswerving in your commitment to your church, you must demonstrate an abundance of flexibility in dealing with your members. The roles that you will be asked to fill may change ten times in one day. At the end of each day, you may not know if you are coming or going!

Action-Oriented and Patient

Traditional churches need pastors who take initiative and lead the people to new challenges. The churches must be shaken from their complacency with the possibilities of God. Traditional churches need pastors who have patience, who can wait on God's timing when it seems that nothing is happening. Traditional churches need pastors who have the wisdom to know when to move and when to wait.

Sensitive and Tough-skinned

Pastors, don't you love it when you have just been through a round of criticisms and a well-meaning church member tells you to get your act together? "Pastor, you just got to have tough skin. You can't let everything hurt you."

Yet before the week is over, you may be taken to task for your insensitivity in not visiting someone. This particular church member may even articulate that you are just not sensitive enough.

Such is the tension that is, and will continue to be, a part of your life. Certain occasions will call for you to have the hide of a rhino, while others will demand that you be sensitive and caring.

How do we reconcile the two demands upon your life? You don't. You recognize that the tension will be ever present, and that God will provide for all of your needs for each and every occasion (Phil. 4:19).

Ambitious and Content

You must have a desire to see your church grow, to reach new heights. You need to set ambitious goals and challenge your people to meet them. You must believe that the God you serve is a God of miracles, and that He will work miracles in your church.

Yet you must be content with what may seem like the pace of a snail. And you can't get discouraged because your church is not Willow Creek, Saddleback, or even the bigger church a few miles away.

You must be ambitious, yet you must be content. It is a paradox. But it is a paradox with which the apostle Paul successfully dealt (compare Phil. 3:14; 4:12). So can you.

Traditional and Contemporary

You must lead your church to reach a contemporary world. Some of the methods must change if that possibility is to ever become a reality. But you must also be willing and even eager to hold on to the traditions that really matter.

Your church is to "become all things to all men so that by all possible means [it] might save some" (1 Cor. 9:22). But your church must not "conform . . . to the pattern of this world" (Rom. 12:2). You must lead your church to be in the world but not of the world.

Encouragement, Hope . . . and Promise

Your role as the leader of a traditional church is not an easy one. Indeed, it is an impossible role without the strength of the Lord.

I am in contact with traditional church pastors and staff members across the nation. I would never minimize the conflict, struggles, and pain that I see in many of these churches.

But something is happening. A fresh wind is blowing. Churches once declared comatose and terminal are now seeing new life. It is the wind of revival that is changing churches from decline to growth. The Holy Spirit is giving a new beginning to churches that once seemed hopeless.

Chuck and I wrote this book out of the conviction that you needed to hear about this new promise. We have prayed that these words would reach pastors, staff members, and lay persons who most needed to hear words of encouragement and hope.

Many years ago, I was a fairly successful corporate banker in a large bank holding company. I considered my place in the world significant, especially since I was continuing a long banking tradition in my family.

But then God began to speak. He started giving me a hunger for preaching and shepherding. He was calling me to be a pastor. The call was nearly irresistible, but I fought it for a while.

Finally, on an early summer day in 1982 I received a call that the seven-year-old son of Lynn and Elaine Clowers was not doing well after heart surgery. Partly because our church was without a pastor, and partly because I loved the family, I dropped everything I was doing to rush to the hospital.

At the moment I arrived at the hospital, my little buddy, Brian Clowers, died. The presence of God was unmistakable in the room. Not only had the Lord come to take Brian home, but He had also come to make clear to my stubborn head my call to ministry. Though the words were not audible, the call was clear: "Thom, ministering to families like the Clowers and reaching and preaching is My will for your life. Will you obey?"

Within a few months, I resigned my job and sold my house and furniture. My family and I headed to seminary in complete confidence that the God who called us would provide for our every need.

My God has been faithful. Sure, there have been struggles, heartaches, critics, and doubts. But my God has never let me down.

You have been called. You are as certain of your call as you are your salvation. My friend, God has not called you to a ministry of futility; He has called you to a ministry of fulfillment.

The traditional church is a challenge, but the church is God's people whom we are called to serve and to love. You will not only meet the challenge, but you are yet to see the most fruitful days of your ministry. My promise? No, God's promise: "Being confident of this, that he who began a good work in you will carry on to completion until the day of Christ Jesus" (Phil. 1:6).

To help you get started on the vision cycle, we have provided a worksheet on the next page. Feel free to use it as you think about ways to address each phase.

God's best to you, my friend. Chuck and I may not know you by name, but we have already prayed for you. The elephant is large, but it can be eaten. May we feast together!

NOTES

1. Cited in Keith Hinson, "Revival! It's Coming Soon to America, Conference Leaders Believe," *Facts & Trends,* November, 1993, 1.

2. Ibid.

3. C. Peter Wagner, *Churches That Pray* (Ventura, Calif: Regal, 1993), 128.

4. Ibid.

Vision Cycle Worksheet

In the blanks, list ideas that might help your church move through that phase of the vision cycle.

3. *Rekindling the Vision*

_____

_____

_____

2. *Unleashing the Church*

_____

_____

_____

4. *Ministry and Growth*

_____

_____

_____

VISION CYCLE

1: *Outward Focus*

_____

_____

_____

5: *Organization and Structure*

_____

_____

_____

OTHER RESOURCES AVAILABLE FROM THOM RAINER
AND CHUCK LAWLESS:

Surprising Insights from the Unchurched (Zondervan, 2002) by
Thom Rainer
> A look at what the "formerly unchurched" tell us about
> what brought them to church.

The Bridger Generation (Broadman and Holman, 1999) by Thom
Rainer
> A description of the "bridger generation" (born 1977-
> 1994) and what effective churches are doing to reach
> them.

Effective Evangelistic Churches (Broadman and Holman, 1995)
by Thom Rainer
> A study of evangelistically growing churches, describing
> what they're doing to reach the lost.

High Expectation Churches (Broadman and Holman, 1997) by
Thom Rainer
> A follow-up look at assimilation in evangelistic churches,
> showing how these churches are keeping the people they
> reach.

The Unchurched Next Door (Zondervan, available October 2003)
by Thom Rainer
> Newest research on the unchurched, including a proposed
> scale to evaluate the spiritual state of non-believers.

*Discipled Warriors: Growing Healthy Churches that are
Equipped for Spiritual Warfare* (Kregel, 2002) by Chuck Lawless
> A look at the relationship between spiritual warfare and
> church growth, including a proposed model of a healthy
> church that threatens the enemy.

Spiritual Warfare: Biblical Truth for Victory (Lifeway, 2001) by Chuck Lawless
> Co-authored with John Franklin, a nine-week group Bible study that guides believers to put on the armor of God; a video teaching series is also available.

Serving in Your Church Prayer Ministry (Zondervan, 2003) by Chuck Lawless
> A small group study for developing an effective prayer ministry in your church.

Making Disciples through Mentoring (Church Growth Institute, 2002) by Chuck Lawless
> Eight-week inductive Bible study based on the lives of Paul and Timothy designed to enlist and equip mentors

- If you are interested in a church consultation, contact the Lawless Group at www.thelawlessgroup.com.
- If you are interested in a church health survey that Dr. Rainer and Dr. Lawless have produced, visit the website for ChurchCentral, Inc., at www.churchcentral.com.
- If you are interested in a congregational survey for a pastor search committee, contact Church Central at the above address.